Age of
Invisible
Machines

Age of Invisible Machines

A Practical Guide to Creating a Hyperautomated Ecosystem of Intelligent Digital Workers

Robb Wilson
with Josh Tyson

WILEY

Published by John Wiley & Sons, Inc., Hoboken, New Jersey.
Published simultaneously in Canada.

For general information on our other products and services or for technical support, please contact our Customer Care Department within the United States at (800) 762-2974, outside the United States at (317) 572-3993 or fax (317) 572-4002.

Wiley also publishes its books in a variety of electronic formats. Some content that appears in print may not be available in electronic formats. For more information about Wiley products, visit our web site at www.wiley.com.

Library of Congress Cataloging-in-Publication Data:

Names: Wilson, Robb, author.
Title: Age of invisible machines : a practical guide to creating a hyperautomated
    ecosystem of intelligent digital workers / Robb Wilson.
Description: First edition. | Hoboken, NJ : Wiley, [2023] | Includes index.
Identifiers: LCCN 2022025468 (print) | LCCN 2022025469 (ebook) | ISBN
    9781119899921 (cloth) | ISBN 9781119899945 (adobe pdf) | ISBN
    9781119899938 (epub)
Subjects: LCSH: Information technology—Economic aspects. | Organizational
    change. | Artificial intelligence.
Classification: LCC HC79.I55 W5666 2023 (print) | LCC HC79.I55 (ebook) |
    DDC 658.4/038—dc23/eng/20220718
LC record available at https://lccn.loc.gov/2022025468
LC ebook record available at https://lccn.loc.gov/2022025469

Cover Design and Image: by north™
SKY10035151_080822

*I'd like to dedicate this book to the people of Ukraine—
so many of whom have become trusted colleagues, friends,
and family over the course of this journey. I'll be donating the first
year of proceeds from this book to Ukraine.*

Contents

Preface

By Josh Tyson

I came to *Age of Invisible Machines* with a solid understanding of the technologies involved in hyperautomation but only a vague notion of how they fit together. Most of this knowledge was seeded in 2012, when I began working as managing editor of *UX Magazine*, the world's longest-running publication for the experience design community, and Robb Wilson, as the owner of *UXM*, had a mythical aura about him.

Given that Robb is a pioneering force in the burgeoning field of experience design, colleagues talked about his ideas and achievements with a mix of awe and affection. Robb had written an early book on effective interface design and had been tapped by Apple to create one of the first iPad apps. He'd already been refining his own conversational AI machine named Cybil for more than 10 years. Apparently, he'd even been nominated for an Academy Award for his work in film. Bursting with big ideas that came rolling down the pike at a steady clip, he was running multiple international start-ups and divided his time between Denver and Kyiv. I rarely saw Robb, but he was always there.

A couple of years ago, I seized an opportunity to spelunk the elusive Robb's mind, helping to refine a white paper about hyperautomation that quickly mushroomed into this book. I was astounded, not only by the complexity and scope of hyperautomation as Robb describes it but also that he was able to come up with an accessible solution for the problems within. Imagine the power of an open system that connects all of the data points (and data stores) within an organization. Anyone can use the platform to sequence a host of disruptive technologies without having to write code, which means anyone can leverage data and create better-than-human automations at every level of society via an interface—conversation—that requires no training.

Named by the tech research and consulting firm Gartner, "hyperautomation" is an inevitable market state and also a convoluted, hairy affair. The deeper I've delved into it, the more I've noticed similar systems in nature. On a hike, for instance, I'll notice how the elegant balance of the individual elements in a healthy forest—the spongy moss, the immovable stones, towering trees—creates a wholly immersive experience made possible by an invisible network sprawling underfoot in every direction. Called "mycelium," this fungal network connects 92% of plant families. The symbiotic relationship between mycelium and plants is called "mycorrhiza"; plants provide the fungi with sugars while the fungi transfers nutrients and water from the soil. The mycorrhiza runs through a network that can spread for miles. All of this goes largely unnoticed—but without it, there'd be no splendor.

Ecosystems for achieving and maintaining hyperautomation are similar. A complex network of technology is orchestrated out of sight in order to give users the ability to harness its power without having to think about how to use it. Similar to the sharing of nutrients, this network connects every department within an organization to the same set of resources that can be called upon by anyone who needs to use them. If you think of problem-solving with technology as running up a hill, hyperautomation allows you to cruise to the top at a steady clip. You don't need to wrestle with clunky graphical user interfaces, you don't have to navigate switchbacks between apps, and you don't have to stop everything and search for the right password.

Designing these digital ecosystems is heavy, complex work, and there's an inverse relationship between the evolution of the simplicity of the experiences people have with technology and the evolution of the complexity required to achieve that simplicity. It's actually a relationship that's been playing out in experience design for decades, where the goal is to create interactions that are as frictionless as possible. Whether spoken or typed, conversation reduces friction better than any other interface. The more intuitive and easy to use a piece of technology is, the more alluring it becomes—and the more complicated it is to create.

The pandemic has sealed the trend of people's primary interactions with organizations—as both customers and employees—being digital in nature. According to Gartner, businesses can gain a sizable competitive advantage in the era of remote work and distributed customers by combining multi-experience, customer experience, employee experience, and user experience into something they call total experience (TX). Using conversational interfaces can maximize impact across a full spectrum of experiences and greatly assist efforts to achieve hyperautomation.[1]

In this regard, conversational AI represents a massive step forward. If users can simply converse with technology, the pain points designers continually have to wrangle with disappear. Of course, the complexity underfoot grows considerably. We'll explore both facets of this inverse relationship: what's possible through achieving hyperautomation and the massive amount of orchestration required to bring those possibilities to life.

Even though a few companies are already achieving, maintaining, and accelerating hyperautomation, much of what Robb describes in this book is still on the verge of taking flight. Similarly, as we worked on the book, the finish line would often recede, the topic ever expanding. There's so much to cover, and the learning process can be very different from the doing process. I've come to think of this book as more of a living document. It's the completed product you're reading now, but it's also connected to a growing library of information, resources, and tools available online at invisiblemachines.ai or via the QR codes you'll find throughout the text.

No matter what your level of experience is with this kind of technology, make no mistake that this is a clarion call announcing an inevitable and rapidly approaching evolution that will upend our relationship with machines. Our goal is to give you the perspective, practical advice, and strategy necessary to remain on firm ground as everything around us changes in ways we're still imagining. These changes are already under way, and the leaders of tomorrow are hard at work today, bringing their organizations closer to hyperautomation.

Acknowledgments

I've been collecting the many ideas, experiences, and stories that went into this book for decades, and getting them wrestled out of my head and onto bookshelves fell on the capable shoulders of Elias Parker, this project's producer and developmental editor. Many thanks for your commitment to seeing this project through. Thank you also to Josh Tyson for helping give these many ideas, experiences, and stories structure and a voice on paper. Hearty high-fives to Jordan Ratner, Alison Harshberger, Mariia Platonova, Jeff Steen, Sofija Mitrovic, the wonderful team at Wiley, and The Editrice, Kirsten Janene-Nelson. Additional thanks to Melody Ossola for your visual designs and bynorth.no for design work on the cover. My journey in conversational AI has brought me into contact with so many great people, incredible opportunities, and sizeable challenges, and *Age of Invisible Machines* isn't the product of just one person, it's the sum of many parts.

A special thank-you to my business partners, Daisy and Rich Weborg, and Kevin Fredrick. Huge thanks all-around to Michael Bevz, Lance Christmann, Jonathan Anderson, Petro Tarasenko, Helen and Antony Peklo, Natalia and Andrey Nikitenko, and the entire family of amazing people at OneReach.ai (who've been diligently building the best conversational AI platform in the world for many, many years now). Thank you to our customers and partners for recognizing the power of our approach long before Gartner and others came along—especially Sherry Comes, former IBM Watson Distinguished Engineer and CTO. Thank you to the old Effective UI crew and the community of authors and readers we've built up at *UX Magazine* over the years.

My eternal gratitude goes to the powerful women I've known throughout my life, including my beautiful daughters: Sid, Cole, Katie, Melly, and Quinn. Opa (or "billing"), you rock. Mom, thank you for everything. Sasha, thank you for doing this with me. I love you. Thank you to my amazing siblings: Holly, Burt, and Ernie. Finally, thank you, Marshall McLuhan, for setting my evolving worldview into motion so many years ago.

Introduction

Conversational AI, My White Whale

By Robb Wilson

Call me Ishmael.

Actually, please don't.

Like Captain Ahab in *Moby-Dick*, I've spent many a waking hour in heated pursuit of a powerful and elusive white whale: conversational AI. For lingering days, months, and years I've chased this steely beast on the horizon. I was frequently knocked off course by the complexity and newness of the various associated technologies, but I kept up the chase on both sides of land and over all sides of earth (as Melville would say).

For me, this obsession began as an early practitioner in the field of experience design. I noticed that the absolute worst experiences people were routinely having with machines were conversational in nature: purgatorial voice automated call centers and feeble chatbots trying to solve problems online and wreaking havoc on user trust with their inefficiency. Lifting users and organizations out of the seemingly infinite shitbot doldrums seemed like the true white whale of experience design.

It was easy to understand why much of the focus in experience design has been put on creating graphical UIs that draw users in and give them rewarding experiences—wherein complex interactions with machines were easier to manage. Our interactions with computers have been screen based for ages, and as those screens have reached higher definition, been reduced in size, and become touch activated, new opportunities to empower and delight have emerged. I've seen some impressive graphical UIs over the years, but there's a ceiling on how much complexity you can condense into a purely visual interface.

On the other hand, in exploring conversational interfaces I realized that nothing could make interactions with machines easier than using our most natural forms of communication. Speech and text are methods for sharing information that nearly everyone on the planet can leverage without special training. There's no need for users to scour a top navigation or figure out what certain icons mean if they can simply converse with the machine functioning underneath the cumbersome GUI. It was clear to me that if conversational AI could fulfil its promise, it would effectively mask the machinations, making the machine invisible.

***

I've now been talking about talking to machines for decades. I recently found myself having a familiar conversation over coffee with the CEO of a publicly traded tech company. Once again, I was hitting on the ways conversational AI and, more broadly, hyperautomation will destroy the status quo.

> *"Putting technology to work will be as simple as asking for its help."*
> *"Using conversation to engage machines' vast problem-solving powers can literally make anyone a technologist."*
> *"Humans will be able to leverage advanced technology without a formal understanding of how to create and deploy software."*
> *"Eventually, we'll even put technology to work by having software build new software."*

The CEO smiled and said it all sounded amazing, but I could tell the immediacy wasn't hitting home. This person helms a company that, at the time of our conversation, was managing projects to build machines for Slack and Teams so as to make their own apps available through those conversational interfaces. I was left waiting to see if he'd realize that his organization is literally undermining their own platform's graphical UI in an effort to accommodate a conversational one.

There have been attempts to scale GUIs, such as SharePoint and Salesforce, but they ultimately revealed the hard truth that a UI with a hundred tabs designed by as many people is even worse to navigate than it sounds. No doubt, one of the biggest reasons Microsoft is moving from SharePoint to Teams is the scalability of a conversational interface that's connected to everything. Customers and employees alike can interact with a company through one portal that ties together and obscures the sausage factory behind the scenes.

Really, the missing link in the creation and widespread adoption of strategies for achieving hyperautomation is a scalable interface. Graphical UIs will never scale to meet the requirements of hyperautomation. This goes well beyond the issue of being too cluttered and overwhelming; it's often the very processes graphical UIs render that need to be automated the most. Conversational AI is the missing link, the infinitely scalable interface. Not only does it handily obscure the mess of systems (and graphical UIs) running behind the scenes, it also binds your ecosystem, creating a feedback loop that can evolve automations for all your users—customers and employees.

Companies such as Lemonade and Ant Group (formerly Ant Financial) are already leveraging conversational AI and hyperautomation to fundamentally alter their respective industries. For this CEO I was conversing with, a frightening realization is waiting around the corner: once wider adoption is resolved, conversational interfaces will undoubtedly scale in ways that will completely obscure graphical UIs.

In the course of building a platform for leveraging conversational AI I've come to realize that it's really a combination of three key technologies: conversational user interfaces, composable architecture, and no-code rapid application programming. In essence this trinity is truly the white whale of experience design. It furthers the frictionless conversational interface to a point where software creation becomes democratized. Instead of focusing on the experience of *using* software, code-free allows us to elevate our efforts to designing the conversational experience of *creating* software using composable architecture. Not only do these component technologies elevate UX design to new heights, they can do the same for humanity, ensuring everyone has access to technology and can easily put it to use: technology that doesn't leave anyone behind.

When the automation of your organization's external and internal operations are leveraged through conversational AI, anyone can create and iterate software solutions on their own. Conversational AI, orchestrated alongside other disruptive technologies on an open platform, can create an ecosystem that allows your team members to work collaboratively on automating tasks and processes in ways that people alone could never achieve. Conversational AI gives customers infinitely more rewarding interactions with your organization while also giving your team members an entirely new paradigm within which to work.

The requirements for this level of automation—hyperautomation—create a scenario where the various elements of experience design become part of a rapidly moving feedback loop. For lack of a more creative term, this represents a kind of hyperUX. The energy previously poured into designing around the limitations of graphic UIs now gets poured into designing for an infinitely scalable conversational interface. The architecture of these experiences requires extensive journey mapping, and those maps become living documents that evolve alongside the experiences. Extensive research and analytics can happen in real time as the people inside your organization watch users moving though experiences as they unfold. And, unlike what happens in our current reality when machines inevitability get stuck, the overall hyperUX experience can continually be rewarding because it's designed to have humans jump in and assist whenever needed. This creates an environment that's more agile than Agile, where code-free interactions with machines allow for iterations and improvements being made constantly.

This might sound far-fetched to anyone who's been held hostage by the sluggish development cycles of their key vendors, but in an ecosystem built for hyperautomating you truly can pull in any piece of technology and make significant changes to any aspect of a user's experience at a moment's notice. I've seen many high-minded projects get dragged through protracted development processes only to stumble down into "release and regret" existence. At its best, building software is a creative process. By applying the strategies and techniques described in this book, you can reach a place where the creative people within your organization can manage the process of software creation from end to end.

If you, like me, have also chased after conversational AI, by now you've likely recognized that doing it the wrong way feels eerily like Ahab's fate: his ship split in two by a forceful beast he never properly reckoned with, he finds himself tied to that force and dragged out to sea. I'm still astonished by the fact that I'm now able to swim alongside my white whale. Taken together in a swirling mass, conversational AI and hyperautomation become something beautiful and monstrous and beguiling. This endeavor doesn't amount to pursuing a trophy you win with a hundred harpoons. Those who try to conquer these technologies will find their schemes smashed to bits. The trick is to be nimble and swift, riding the waves alongside them as everything churns madly around you. The prize of "catching" conversational AI matters so much because of what it symbolizes: You've learned to harness conversational UI, composable architecture, and no-code creation by creating a strategic environment where everyone can use technology effectively and no one is left behind (or out to sea).

In the pages to follow, we'll take a deep dive into the complexity of this new realm. By sharing with you everything I've learned, I want to help your organization swim with the speed, strength, and flexibility necessary to propel itself forward in choppy waters. This will be an arduous and complex journey fraught with difficult decisions, but it will also give you the chance to reflect on the outdated processes and systems that have been holding you back. Regardless of whether this sounds appealing to you or horrifying, the bottom line is it's time to take the plunge. In this space I'll share the perspective of my journey over the course of 20+ years. If you're going to do this, it's crucial to have a point of view, so I'll lend you mine.

PART I

Imagining an Ecosystem of Intelligent Digital Workers

As I've already hinted in the Introduction, creating an ecosystem that supports achieving a state of hyperautomation is a monumental task, and you'll want to approach it with solid foundational knowledge. In Part I, we'll take a look at the current landscape (as of this writing), dispel some of the common myths associated with conversational AI, and start to paint a picture of what successfully achieving hyperautomation looks like. With technology this all-encompassing and powerful, it's also crucial to bear in mind the myriad ethical concerns that will arise. These orchestrated technologies will upend our world in rather sudden ways, transforming established chunks of our daily routines. This work must be done with more than just good intentions; we must pay close attention to the shifting outcomes of those good intentions as things begin to accelerate. And accelerate they will. We are more or less at the starting point; from here we can set a trajectory that benefits everyone, leaving no one behind.

Massive opportunities are waiting for the organizations that take these efforts seriously, and that are willing to make the sacrifices of letting go of outdated systems and structures. There is a world within reach where everyone has access to technology and no one is left behind—where soul-sucking jobs are a thing of the past, and companies are increasingly self-driving. In this world, people are free to work together on the most interesting, creative problems, and not only within the confines of large companies. The strategic application of conversational AI to achieve a state of hyperautomation is just a means to that end—to that place where technology benefits everyone equally.

This is the book about how to get to that world. It's about how to get your team and company to organize and operate in ways that are highly conducive to achieving and maintaining a state of hyperautomation, which is what allows your organization to become increasingly self-driving. Being in a state of hyperautomation is not unlike someone in a state of ketosis—having starved a body of carbohydrates to burn for energy so it starts burning fat for fuel instead. Hyperautomation means reorganizing your organization's insides (and likely starving it of outdated tools and processes) so that it can exist in a far more potent and efficient state. To whet this new appetite, let's first explore some scenarios of where hyperautomation can take your organization (and the world).

CHAPTER 1

Hyperautomation Is Already Here

I don't want to scare you, but this book comes with an ominous warning: the status quo is a death sentence. Most modern organizations are run using systems and strategies that will seem almost comically outdated a few short years from now. That's because the strategic orchestration of technologies described in this book—deep learning, blockchain and code-free development tools—will do a lot more than disrupt the ways we're accustomed to dealing with technology; that strategic orchestration will obliterate existing models.

We're living in an era when technology moves in exponential leaps and bounds, every day growing more powerful, more pervasive, and more sophisticated. It's no coincidence that 90% of all the data in existence was created over the past two years[1], but in many ways this wealth of information represents a failure. To say it's being poorly leveraged is a bit of an understatement, but all of this is about to change.

The technologies surrounding conversational AI are heading toward a point of convergence that will fundamentally alter our relationship with machines. Already, the experiences customers and employees have with businesses are being reshaped by the hallmarks of this convergence—putting those massive stores of data into action in ways that have upended entire industries. This might sound hyperbolic—especially given the substandard chatbot experiences endemic to much of the automation happening in the world at present—but it's not.

The reason that conversational AI in particular feels like a lot of talk is simply because it hasn't been more widely adopted—yet. The technology surrounding conversational AI has become highly sophisticated, but that hasn't changed the fact that people don't like pogo-sticking between 10 different machines. For example, let's say you log on to your home security system website to cancel service. Asking their chatbot a question drops you down a funnel of FAQ menus where you learn, five minutes in, that cancelations can't be handled online. When you next call the accounts department, you're confronted by a series of voice automations that feels like another funnel drop, so you start stamping "0" hoping for a shortcut to a live agent. Crap experiences like this can feel less productive than just waiting on hold and hoping you can remember the security PIN you created five years ago.

The "I don't have time—I'll do it the long way" mindset is symptomatic of the lackluster conversational experiences users are accustomed to having with machines. But that's starting to change. One of the key elements of this convergence of technologies surrounding conversational AI involves intelligent and evolving ecosystems designed for accelerated automation powered by one of humankind's oldest adaptations: conversation. Make no mistake, it's not that conversational AI isn't going anywhere—it's going everywhere.

Groundbreaking as they've been, recent innovations such as Alexa and Google Home hardly qualify as conversational AI. Asking smart speakers to issue weather reports, set a timer, or play a song are very limited and immature applications of conversational AI, though they hint at its nascent power. Smart speakers have completely upended the speaker industry, to the point where it might be difficult to find a new speaker for sale that doesn't have built-in conversational capabilities. But how powerful does a smart speaker become when it's not limited to the things that Siri or Alexa can do? What happens when you can ask your speaker to play "Mr. Roboto" by Styx and then follow up with another request: "I want to buy a copy of the book that Marc Maron mentioned during the intro to his podcast today. I don't remember the title but see if there's a copy available from Powell's before looking on Amazon."

What will happen is, a few minutes later, a text message could appear on your phone with a link showing a hardcover copy of *Camera Man* by Dana Stevens available on Powells.com. By replying, "Yes. Please buy" via text, you'd be communicating with the same interface that you initially spoke to—an umbrella conversational interface that has become your primary interaction point with most of the technology in your life. Once this scenario is possible, you won't think of technology in terms of different apps, because you'll rarely need to open and interact with an app. *Domo arigato, Mr. Roboto.*

Of course, human conversation is broader than the spoken word, as we have many ways of communicating our thoughts and needs. Humans frequently incorporate gestures, facial expressions, visual aids, and sounds in conversation. As such, conversational AI encompasses a full breadth of what I call "multi-turn" or "multimodal" interactions. Because they are part of an interconnected ecosystem, these multimodal interactions can leverage those massive stores of data we're continually creating—unearthing massive opportunities for personalization and precision.

To explain what I mean by multi-turn or multimodal: having a text conversation with an invisible machine might include that machine showing you part of a video to illustrate a point. If you're asking it to analyze a spreadsheet or data, it can draw you a graph on the fly to help visualize data points. If the interaction is ongoing and you're about to start driving, the interface can move to voice command. These multimodal experiences mirror normal parts of conversations between people, and that sophistication enables humans to wield technological functions and capabilities using our most natural interface. These micro UIs, as you might call them, are dialogue-driven and, just like human conversations, they can include all kinds of audio and visual aids and even haptic cues.

You could never have an experience this seamless and efficient while digging through nested tabs or apps—and many of the world's leading companies are coming around to this fact. Salesforce didn't just acquire Slack. Their CEO has openly admitted that they are rebuilding their entire organization around Slack. Microsoft is doing similarly with Teams: they're betting that an integrated communication platform and a unifying conversational interface—one machine that connects to everything—will benefit customers, employees, and organizations in big ways.

When this level of natural conversation becomes the primary interface between machines and the humans using them, the machine becomes invisible as the interface disappears. This line of thinking should be familiar to most experience design practitioners. One of the hallmarks of successful experience design is an interface that gets out of the way. The further the interface recedes into the background during an experience, the more frictionless that experience becomes. This lightens a user's cognitive load and helps them to get what they need from the technology more effectively (though it also represents a massive amount of orchestration behind the scenes).

With conversational AI, interfacing with machines no longer requires that we adapt to the way they communicate, which dramatically reduces friction in our experiences with machines and software. Conversational AI will go anywhere and everywhere—meaning that invisible machines will be, for lack of a less grandiose term, omnipresent. You'll be able to turn to your phone, any nearby smart speaker, or any voice-enabled appliance and enlist the help of an invisible machine. This ties into another element of this convergence, which involves sequencing technology so that it can react and adapt to individual situations. Invisible machines galore, connected to ecosystems built for optimized problem solving. Add it all up, and you get something called hyperautomation.

Hyperautomation Minus the Hype

Sequencing disruptive, advanced technologies to work in concert is something Gartner calls hyperautomation, and it's as intense as it sounds. Gartner coined the term in 2019; by their estimation, "Technology is now on the cusp of moving beyond augmentation that replaces a human capability and into augmentation that creates superhuman capabilities." I've noticed people finding Gartner's definition to be a bit loose. If you tighten the definition to specifically require that automation results in producing better than human experiences, then there's less confusion around how hyperautomation is different from automation. Presume hyperautomation to result in better experiences, not just automated experiences, and that's how I'll be using the term in this book.

Implementing a strategy for hyperautomation is a massive undertaking that requires cooperation from every department within your organization. But you're not helpless in the face of hyperautomation. You can't succeed by resigning yourself to hyperautomation. It's not something you have to succumb to. You can take charge, but first you have to surrender many of the old ways of doing things.

Hyperautomating isn't a space for concrete plans, flexibility is the name of the game, and you need an open platform that gives you control of the tools and software you use when automating experiences.

OneReach.ai was founded more than 10 years ago, with a dedication to breaking down conversational AI into patterns that can be sequenced to hyperautomate the work that needs to be done. I've spent the majority of my life trying to improve the ways people and machines communicate with each other. Hyperautomation represents a massive leap forward on both sides of these interactions. I believe hyperautomation has the potential for disruption on a scale similar to the advent of the printing press, the industrial revolution, and the dawn of the computer age itself. What's different is that the rate of change will most likely be much faster.

Hyperautomation is really an application strategy that goes beyond the development of AI and into how you sequence it with other disruptive technologies to solve complex problems as part of an organization-wide experience strategy. As you'll discover in the "Tools and Architecture" section in this book, technology exists right now that can help you move toward hyperautomating business processes, workflows conversations, and tasks to offer better-than-human experiences (or what my team is calling BtHX)—but most companies haven't yet tapped into it.

As Harvard Business School professor Marco Iansiti said about hyperautomation: "A lot of people think of this as disruption, like the taxi industry . . . being disrupted by Uber. It's not disruption. . . . Firms have been designed with management and labor since the Industrial Revolution. This is a fundamental change in the means of production, and it's affecting every industry across the board."

It's common for organizations to focus on disruptive technology in myopic ways—in this case, seeing automation as a means to handle simple tasks on human terms, such as automating a coffee maker so that it brews a fresh pot of coffee at 8:45 a.m. What if, instead, the coffee pot was part of a better-than-human experience that not only adjusts the time it brews coffee and the amount it brews, but also cross references company calendars and brews an extra-strong pot of coffee in anticipation of a client coming straight to the office from an international flight. Better yet, imagine a nimble financial institution streamlining operations and eliminating overhead by hyperautomating tasks such as approving loans, conducting credit score checks, and dispensing financial advice.

This is how China's Ant Group operates. They are a hyperautomated powerhouse whose mobile payment service boasts more than 450 million active users. (Apple Pay sits at about 12 million.)[2]

When we think about AI we often think about the notion of singularity—the hypothetical point in time when a powerful superintelligence will surge past all human intelligence. There's also the notion of machines gaining artificial general intelligence (AGI) and, thus, the ability to learn any intellectual task that humans can. These versions of superintelligence won't be the product of some super algorithm.

The perception of singularity or AGI is more likely to emerge from an ecosystem of algorithms and technologies sequenced in intelligent ways to work in concert and likely would be made up of contributions from different pieces of software engineered all over the world. These ecosystems of algorithms and sequenced technologies are very similar to the ones I'll describe in this book.

While the arrival of singularity could be many decades away, we've already quietly passed a significant milestone. Users are now having experiences with some conversational AI that are far more rewarding than what their human counterparts offer (BtHX). For evidence, I'll turn again to Ant Group, which told *MIT Technology Review* that customer satisfaction with their chatbots had surpassed human performance. "There are many, many chatbot companies in Silicon Valley," Yuan Qi, Ant's vice president and AI chief scientist, noted at the time. "We are the only one that can say, confidently, [our chatbots perform] better than human beings."[3]

There's also the example of Lemonade, a tech-minded start-up that has disrupted the rental insurance market with low prices, a program for donating premium surplus money to charity, and a better-than-human customer-facing conversational AI.

"The biggest thing that pushed me to convert to Lemonade was the utterly charming AI chatbot," Juliette van Winden wrote in a Medium post dedicated to their chatbot, Maya. "24/7, 365, day or night, Maya is there to answer any questions to guide the user through the sign-up process. Unlike the drag of signing up with other providers, it took me a total of two minutes to walk through all the steps with Maya. . . . What intrigued me the most, is that it didn't feel like I was chatting with a bot. Maya is funny and charismatic—which made the exchange feel authentic."[4]

We'll explore all sorts of scenarios in the "How Hyperautomation Can Change the World" chapter of this section. But for now, imagine this kind of reality playing out in another context: Your router goes down. You place a call to your service provider and are guided through all the necessary system checks quickly and elegantly by a conversational app. Or, better yet, how about their hyperautomated ecosystem detects that your router is down and their conversational app reaches out to you before you even notice that you're offline. This is the work of an intelligent digital worker, or IDW. Far more capable than a chatbot, the IDW is connected to this service provider's ecosystem, which is a network of interdependent technologies, processes, and people. This customer-service-oriented IDW reaches out to you because it got an alert from a fellow machine in the maintenance department that your location had lost coverage. The IDW is programmed to isolate and troubleshoot the issue by running background tasks while it speaks with you to verify your account and location. This intelligent digital worker could ask you to send a photo of the blinking lights on your router while it simultaneously looks internally at your connection status. It assesses and course-corrects in seconds and your router is back up and running inside of five minutes. Best part? You didn't have to wait on hold for a human operator, because there are unlimited digital agents at the ready—or because they called you, having detected the issue before you did. After experiencing this kind of BtHX firsthand, you'll never want to go back.

It's always been frustrating for us to watch organizations invest heavily in marketing to get customers in the door and then invest more money in call centers to get them out the door. Hyperautomation can close that gap and make every interaction a customer has with an organization pleasant and fruitful. Literally every interaction with a customer becomes an opportunity.

As conversational AI is sequenced with other technologies to contextualize massive amounts of data within an ecosystem that can give customers and employees access to elevated problem-solving capabilities, the world as we know it will change fundamentally.

In this book we'll explore the components of a robust ecosystem for hyperautomating business processes, workflows, tasks, and communications, along with what a strategy looks like for evolving these ecosystems.

What's important to remember throughout is that the potential created by hyperautomation is so vast that the marketplace advantage can be staggering for companies with these ecosystems already in place. Making the most of this hyperdisruptive moment in history (and not being left behind) requires a holistic undertaking that touches on all aspects of your business. Random acts of technology—like deploying disparate machines that exist in isolation—will underwhelm your workforce and customers, leading to low adoption rates. A fully integrated approach, however, can bring about a totally new paradigm of productivity with unprecedented potential.

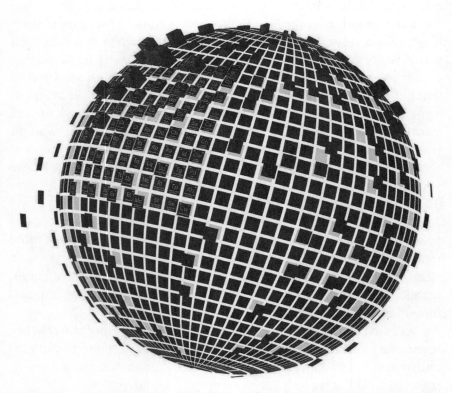

FIGURE 1.1 *An ecosystem of intelligent digital workers. (OneReach.ai)*

"Wow, This Sounds Really Hard"

Hyperautomation is indeed a momentous undertaking. The easiest way to get started is often to automate internally first; start small by automating individual tasks and skills, not entire jobs. The simpler you make your starting point, the sooner you can test and iterate. The sooner you test and iterate, the sooner you can roll out an internal solution. You'll continue testing and iterating on that solution, using the momentum to find new skills to develop, test, iterate on, and deliver. You'll fumble often as you grow legs, but that's part of the process, too. In the realm of hyperautomation, we are more agile than Agile (hyperagile, in a sense). With the right tools and budding ecosystem, the iteration process becomes so speedy that failures are often quick rewards that point to better solutions. Because fixes and new solutions can be tested and deployed quickly and at will, your organization can build on wins and gain speed.

"Iteration" is a term tossed about freely in most enterprise settings, but it's important to remember that the real goal is to be continuously improving. By rolling out internal successes with automation and continually improving on them, you're both demonstrating to everyone in your organization, top to bottom, the process by which hyperautomation will take place—and introducing them to the ecosystem they will eventually call home. In the long term, this will bring you closer to creating and testing customer-facing conversational applications. In the near term, by focusing on helping your team members accomplish more and experience more satisfaction with their jobs, your customers will be rewarded downstream. This isn't the only way to reach the goal of hyperautomation, but it's generally the fastest way to accelerate your path to AI adoption on an organizational level.

Hyperautomation Brings Hyperdisruption

I can't help but reiterate that these changes to business are under way, and they're going to accelerate in astonishing ways. The "hyper" is there for a reason, and the sequencing of disruptive technologies inside ecosystems built for hyperautomation will unleash hyperdisruptions across all industries, emerging suddenly and in ways that we won't always be able to predict. But while the hyper aspects of these disruptions are new, the sequencing of technology to solve complex problems has been with us for centuries.

The printing press is an easy disruption to point to, as it spread information all across medieval Europe and eventually the world in a truly revolutionary manner. But the printing press itself was a variation on presses that were already being used to squeeze grapes for wine and olives for oil. When Gutenberg printed his bible in 1455, it was the product of an orchestration of variations on other disruptive technologies: an oil-based improvement on existing inks, customizations to paper and moveable type originally developed in China, metallurgy, and the press.[5]

It's in our nature to innovate by orchestrating technologies in our favor, and hyperautomation represents a new era wherein anyone with an idea can have a voice. And with that voice, they can orchestrate disruptive technologies to accomplish things others haven't even dreamed of.

As I'll describe in these pages, assembling a diverse team and fostering a culture that champions change are keys to success in a landscape that will be continually disrupted. Embracing change lets you use speed and iteration to offset any fear of failure. Sometimes the best way to learn and make progress is to just start—adopting a practice of failing forward fast. Big changes on top of big changes are on the way, so alarm, urgency, and action are all merited. For those just getting started or who are already up to their necks, rest assured, there are practical ways to achieve hyperautomation.

Printing press–level disruptions will come by the week, not the decade. To help set your bearings, in chapter 5 we'll explore several scenarios for how hyperautomation might rewrite our experiences with technology and change our daily existence in a flash. But first, let's set the record straight on what conversational AI is and isn't.

Key Takeaways

- Hyperautomation is here, and it's already being used by companies such as Ant Group and Lemonade to disrupt two long-standing industries: banking and insurance.
- Once the wider adoption of conversational AI takes hold, our interactions with machines will change fundamentally, ushering in an era of unprecedented technological advancement.
- Hyperautomation isn't something you have to succumb to. You can take charge, but you'll also have to sacrifice many of the old ways of doing things.
- In a world where organizations of all shapes and sizes are hyper-automating, orchestrating disruptive technologies to solve increasingly complex problems will be the order of the day.
- The accelerated orchestration of disruptive forces will create an atmosphere of hyperdisruption, where entire industries will be reimagined on a regular basis.

Visit invisiblemachines.ai for more information on hyper-automation.

CHAPTER 2

What Conversational Artificial Intelligence Is—and Isn't

The resistance to automation and conversational AI has many facets. Much of the pushback relates to the automation of tasks that people don't believe machines can do well or don't trust machines to do at all. As conversational AI and ecosystems for hyperautomating become the norm, however, it will become readily apparent that there are a vast number of tasks and processes that can be automated with great success by machines, so long as those machines have humans in control and guiding the process.

"Automation" refers to tasks humans typically perform being performed instead by machines. By extension, "hyperautomation" is achieved by successfully orchestrating advanced technologies—such as machine learning, composable architecture, computer vision, conversational technologies, and code-free development tools—in order to automate tasks and processes that are outside the capability of humans alone. It's the coordination of advanced technologies to work in concert, to automate with massively enhanced impact.

It's tempting to think of conversational AI as nothing more than a new interface that experience designers can apply their skills to, but it's something much larger than that. Conversational AI represents a vast, emergent set of technologies obscured by layers of hype and misinformation. There's a very reasonable sense of urgency surrounding its adoption and implementation within the business community, but putting it to work requires a fuller understanding of what it actually entails.

In reality, successful implementation of conversational AI requires an open ecosystem built for hyperautomation, where a shared library of information and code-free design tools make high-level automation and continual evolution an everyday thing. While it's possible that this ecosystem can be built using technologies that are part of your existing ecosystem, a sizable evolution will be necessary nonetheless. With hyperautomation your ecosystem moves from being app-based and limited in scalability by disparate graphical user interfaces to skills- and functionality-based, with a unifying conversational interface connecting everything. In order to achieve hyperautomation, interchangeable technologies are sequenced and orchestrated using an open platform that gives you both the freedom to implement the best functionalities from any vendor and the flexibility to iterate on solutions quickly and at will. It's also important that you're able to orchestrate quickly and make continual improvements to those orchestrations. This is really about strategically sequencing technologies inside your ecosystem; hyperautomating means you're doing this quickly while constantly implementing iterative improvements.

When you start thinking about conversational AI in the right way, you begin to see that it's not a piece of technology to be wielded; it's part of a business strategy for building an ecosystem where various technologies are sequenced to automate tasks and processes in ways that surpass what humans alone are capable of. Conversational AI isn't magic, it's just math + logic—and when it's orchestrated properly, it eliminates all communication barriers between humans and machines.

Perhaps the easiest way to illustrate what conversational AI is would be to clarify what it is not. To follow are the truths behind some of the more persistent myths about conversational AI.

Dispelling Common Myths About Conversational Artificial Intelligence

Myth 1. Conversational AI is just talking to machines.

Not even close. Natural language processing (NLP) and natural language understanding (NLU) are actually just two of the smaller pieces of the conversational AI puzzle. Getting computers to the point where they can (a) contextualize the things that people say (NLP) as well as (b) understand the intent behind what's being said and (c) provide useful responses (NLU) required massive leaps in technology, touching on intent recognition, entity recognition, fulfillment, voice-optimized responses, dynamic text-to-speech, machine learning, and contextual awareness. At present, only a handful of organizations are leveraging this technology at high levels and not just because experiences in a state of hyperautomation go beyond the limits of talking and typing—incorporating gestures, facial expressions, visual aids, sounds, and haptic feedback. Behind the scenes, conversational AI relies on a whole stew of technologies and processes, including integrations, task automation, multichannel optimization, conversational design, maintenance and optimization, and real-time analytics and reporting. In that context, comparing NLP/NLU to conversational AI is like comparing a bicycle wheel to an automobile. The same can be said of text-to-speech (TTS) or "read aloud" technology, which converts typed words into audio; and automated speech recognition (ASR), which allows users to speak commands rather than press numbers on a keypad. In fact, the more complex a use case becomes, the less prominently NLP/NLU factors in. A Q&A bot addressing employee health care options is entirely NLP/NLU (e.g., identify question, provide correct answer, done). When automating the process of signing an employee up for the right health plan, however, NLP/NLU plays a limited role. Once it has helped identify that a user wants to sign up for a plan, other technologies and processes swing into action: authentication, gathering personal employee data, generating suggested plans, signing up users for the chosen plan, confirming transactions via email, and so forth. All of these actions require an ecosystem created for automation. Conversational AI is light-years beyond just talking to machines.

Myth 2. Conversational AI is an add-on.

Nope. Conversational AI isn't something you plug in and watch spring to life. Extracting value from conversational AI requires a comprehensive strategy, especially where legacy systems are involved. The good news is that the amount of work and introspection it takes to successfully implement and scale a conversational AI strategy pays dividends in the ways it unifies and improves all facets of an organization.

Myth 3. The goal of conversational AI is to mimic humans.

Humans are capable of amazing things—as a species, we're continually pushing the boundaries of what we can accomplish. But conversational AI isn't human; we're not trying to pretend it's human, and you shouldn't try to make it human. The point of conversational AI and hyperautomation is to unlock the ways sequenced technology can perform services far better than what humans alone are capable of.

Myth 4. This stuff is easy.

It can be challenging to integrate conversational AI into organizational operations. As much as we might be tempted to hurl chatbots at isolated workflows, in reality successful implementation of conversational AI requires an ecosystem built for hyperautomation—where a shared library of information, patterns, and templates join with code-free design tools to produce high-level automation and continual evolution.

Myth 5. You should start big.

Most organizations don't need a large-scale, public-facing deployment—like Bank of America's virtual financial assistant, Erica—to put conversational AI to good use. It's often more effective to begin by working within your organization, automating internal tasks with help from the people who understand those tasks best. Working internally, you can also get a handle on how to sequence technology to complete jobs in more efficient and rewarding ways than humans alone are able to. This will form the groundwork for an ecosystem of conversational AI that can grow to include customers at a point when you're equipped to provide them with optimized experiences. You'll want to start small, simple, and internally—then iteratively advance, expand, and scale.

Myth 6. Business-minded people know enough to pick the best conversational AI platforms.

Given the complexity I've already discussed (not to mention what's to come in subsequent chapters), the business minds in your organization can't make conversational AI decisions alone. This calls for a collaborative effort that draws on expertise from various disciplines within your organization. You'll need input from those who understand the technology you currently have in place, those who have relationships with your customer base, and those who understand the aspects of your business that are ripe for automation. The best way to make sure you acquire the right tools and systems is to develop a fuller understanding of what goes into creating an ecosystem for hyperautomation to live in. Once you have a shared vision of what you want to build, it will be far easier to see which products will truly provide you with valuable solutions. Successful conversational AI platforms emerge from a collaborative effort among key personnel in your organization.

Myth 7. You can do this alone.

Hyperautomation isn't an initiative you can put solely in the hands of any one group in your organization. You need a core team of specialists instituting a process that involves members from every department in your organization. That core team can come from within your organization or the outside world, but its members have to be adept enablers. As they work their own skill-specific roles, they need to always be evangelizing the potential for anyone with a good idea to contribute to the design of automated solutions. Hyperautomation is an all-hands-on-deck journey.

Myth 8. To get conversational AI right you need to hire an expert.

The sequencing of conversational AI in ecosystems built for hyperautomating is still in the inception stage, so there aren't yet expert agencies or hired guns that can get you up to speed with the flip of a switch.

That's not to say that there aren't great partners out there who can help you with elements of hyperautomation. Just note that having others set up everything for you isn't the best use of your investment. Instead, select a partner committed to training your own team in successful implementation methods.

Myth 9. There is one platform to rule them all.

Giant companies such as Amazon, Microsoft, and IBM have very sophisticated products that address certain facets of conversational AI, but none of them has a platform or service that can deliver hyperautomation. What you need is an open system that allows you to leverage a whole host of tools, enabling you to sequence and orchestrate different technologies. Hyperautomation requires a network of elements working together in an evolutionary fashion. To quickly grow your ecosystem, you'll want to try as many solutions as possible as quickly as possible. The best approach is to iterate rapidly—to continually improve by trying out new configurations and isolating the best tools, AIs, and algorithms for your business. Open systems allow you to understand, analyze, and manage the relationships among the moving parts inside your ecosystem, which is crucial when moving toward hyperautomation. Remember, this isn't a race to adopt any specific technology; it's a race to put yourself in the position to adopt as many different technologies as possible.

Myth 10. Phones aren't relevant to hyperautomating.

It's easy to think of conversational AI as a web-based technology, but telephony is where most of its cost-saving attributes are found. While a sizeable number of people spend the majority of their time sitting at a computer, just about everyone carries a smaller computer on their person, all day long. Smartphones have all sorts of capabilities such as SMS, voice, GPS, and banking, which can be leveraged across ecosystems built for sequencing conversational AI.

There's also a large segment of the world's population whose only access to the Internet comes through the less-expensive feature phone or the hybrid smart feature phone. According to Yiwen Wu, a senior analyst at Strategy Analytics, "We estimate the global smartphone user base has risen dramatically from just 30k people in 1994 to 1.00 billion in 2012, and a record 3.95 billion today in June 2021. With an estimated 7.9 billion people in total on the planet in June 2021, it means 50% of the whole world now owns a smartphone."[1]

Also, though call centers are declining in general, they are still very much a viable piece of many businesses around the world. Merijn te Booij—chief marketing officer of Genesys, a contact center technology company—told *Vox* how, in the early days of the pandemic, they "saw a lot of people moving away from digital channels very quickly to the voice channel, trying to get certainty, assurances, empathy, making sure that they got commitments on the enterprise decision."[2] The bottom line is that phones of varying degrees of sophistication are key interface points for ecosystems where conversational AI is being sequenced. They can offer a broader reach and enhanced flexibility, so don't count them out.

Myth 11. You can get to the next level with the system and pretrained bots you already have.

Most organizations that have made attempts at automation via conversational AI are stuck watching disparate chatbots sputter along independently without any meaningful connections to their fellow bots or the organization using them. This is a waste of time and resources that alienates customers and team members alike. For context, Gartner charts most of these out-of-box machines as being both low effort and low value. As you move toward higher effort/value integrations, your capabilities surge from being domain specific with limited channels and response capabilities, to machines that can function more like virtual assistants—capable of data-driven decision-making, working across channels, and behaving proactively. Getting to the much higher level of hyperautomation requires a strategy for building an ecosystem in which this kind of conversational AI thrives. Through the process you might discover that certain elements of your existing ecosystem can become integrated into your evolved ecosystem, but they will never serve as the springboard for the necessary evolution.

Acquiring chatbots that are already set up to automate particular workflows your organization uses might seem like a shortcut to hyperautomation, but it will cost you more time in the long term. As you automate workflows, you're going to find opportunities to improve them.

If your only option is to query the machine's developers with your requests, you're entering a cycle of waiting: waiting on iterations, testing them, and then waiting for updates. This wastes time and kills momentum. You need customizable tools that allow you to make code-free design changes at will—changes you can then test internally and implement quickly. That's the true path to hyperautomation.

Myth 12. You'll improve operations by automating existing workflows.

On the surface, it might seem like the biggest win of conversational AI would be to have it run monotonous tasks in place of humans. While there is some usefulness in that, the real value comes with automating better ways of doing things. For example, let's say you call the IRS following up on a letter they sent you. Your first hurdle is to figure out which of the unintelligible clusters of voice-automated options most closely applies to your situation. Then you repeat that process a few more times as you move through murky layers of their phone tree, unsure if you're headed to the right department and expecting to wait on hold for hours to find out. What if, instead, you were greeted by an intelligent digital worker that could verify your personal information while cross-referencing your recent tax history to infer that you're calling about a letter that was sent last week. What if that IDW could also tell you that the payment you sent was received after the letter was sent, give you a confirmation number, and send you on your way in under five minutes? Within an ecosystem of integrated conversational AI that kind of better-than-human experience can readily be designed and implemented.

Myth 13. This is like any other software build-out.

The waterfall approach to software creation is severely outdated and has sprung countless leaks over the years. If you attempt to apply it within the framework of designing conversational AI solutions, you will drown. Creating an ecosystem for hyperautomation using conversational AI is an iterative process that demands the flexibility of rapid, code-free design tools for the steady deployment of new solutions. Even companies that are used to Agile methodologies should prepare for faster iteration cycles than they might be accustomed to.

Myth 14. You can upload all your organization's stored data and proceed to launch.

If only it were that simple. Accumulating massive amounts of data about your customers and business has never been easier, but extracting the value buried in the heaps is a complex and ongoing endeavor that requires a comprehensive strategy. (And though some may be tempted to address this concern with a plug-and-play approach, note that these methods peak at about 40 precent accuracy, which means most of your data would be wasted.) In order to extract all its value, data needs to be categorized within a framework that makes it an active resource accessible across your entire ecosystem. One of the most potent tools for accelerating these efforts is a scenario where machines query humans within an organization whenever they bump up against the limits of their abilities. Not only can the humans help move the current interaction forward, they can also instruct the machines so that the machines can solve the problem without help in the future.

FIGURE 2.1

Key Takeaways

- As conversational AI becomes commonplace, a vast number of tasks and processes will be automated with great success by machines guided and controlled by humans.

- Success with conversational AI requires an open ecosystem built for hyperautomation, where high-level automation and continual evolution occur daily.

- When orchestrated properly, conversational AI eliminates all communication barriers between humans and machines.

- Before getting started with conversational AI, it's critical to let go of the many common myths associated with it.

Visit invisiblemachines.ai for more information on conversational AI and its pivotal role in hyperautomation.

CHAPTER 3

Competing in the Age of Hyperautomation

Plenty of organizations will be tempted to put off hyperautomation, thinking they don't have the resources for an undertaking that seems so extensive and volatile. But the bottom line is that avoiding the inevitable widespread adoption of hyperautomation puts a company at risk of losing market share. Meanwhile, companies that successfully achieve and maintain hyperautomation put themselves in a league beyond even their nearest competitors.

"Hyperautomation has shifted from an option to a condition of survival," Fabrizio Biscotti, research vice president at Gartner, said in 2021. "Organizations will require more IT and business process automation as they are forced to accelerate digital transformation plans in a post-COVID-19, digital-first world."[1]

Companies that are hyperautomating are not only accomplishing more with less, it's also easier for them to further automate new and more sophisticated processes and tasks. This scenario sets off a force multiplier that sends them on a path toward operational superiority. When companies find their stride with hyperautomation, it becomes exponentially harder for their competitors to reach them.

What Successful Hyperautomation Can Look Like

As a company expands and evolves its ecosystem, it's able to automate more and more tasks of greater and greater complexity.

This increasingly frees people's time to work on more creative endeavors, such as problem solving and automating additional workflows.

I mentioned in chapter 1 that China's Ant Group has upended the global banking industry by hyperautomating internal and customer-facing processes. The fact that they've successfully implemented conversational AI and machine learning has given them a stunning head start. As the 2020s were about to dawn, Ant surpassed the number of customers served by today's largest US banks by more than 10 times—a stat that's even more impressive when you consider that this success came before their fifth year in business. An earlier valuation had already made them worth roughly half as much as JPMorgan Chase, then the world's most valuable financial services company.[2]

There are at least a few core differences that set Ant apart from most other financial institutions—and really, most companies. The connecting theme for these core differences is hyperautomation. For Ant, automation solutions aren't created at random; they're part of an ecosystem of automation technologies that work efficiently in concert.

That Ant is a digital company at its core can be seen in the conception, strategy, and execution of everything they do. "This is just the beginning," CEO Eric Jing wrote in a 2018 *Wall Street Journal* article. "Blockchain, artificial intelligence, cloud computing, the Internet of Things, biometrics, and other technologies are generating more ways to upgrade financial systems to make them more transparent, secure, inclusive and sustainable."[3]

Their success in hyperautomating is aptly summed up by *Harvard Business Review*: "There are no workers in [Ant's] 'critical path' of operating activities. AI runs the show. There is no manager approving loans, no employee providing financial advice, no representative authorizing consumer medical expenses. And without the operating constraints that limit traditional firms, Ant Group can compete in unprecedented ways and achieve unbridled growth and impact across a variety of industries."[4]

As technology continues to evolve at a rapid pace, most companies struggle to keep up with the pace of change. The companies with an edge right now will likely leave their competitors trailing far behind. Getting that edge is not as difficult as it sounds; in fact, it can be quite an exciting journey. But it requires a fresh way of thinking.

Instead of creating solutions that require an omniscient designer or team, focus on building a framework for solving complexity.

Thinking of automation as being a direct solution for a particular complex problem can be daunting. But when you think of automation as a framework for solving complex problems, it becomes far more flexible and applicable. Variety can solve complexity.

COVID-19 Has Accelerated Everything

I'd be remiss to not also point out that the COVID-19 pandemic accelerated the use of and need for this type of automation. According to McKinsey Analytics, "The pressure for organizations to adopt AI was already mounting before [COVID-19] as the technology delivered returns to early adopters. [The crisis] has only elevated the technology's prominence, with many companies using AI to quickly triage the vast challenges they face and set a new course for their employees, customers, and investors in an uncertain, rapidly evolving landscape."[5]

While hyperautomation creates a wealth of opportunity, it also poses a genuine threat to businesses. Companies that are unfamiliar with the scope of this process—or are implementing fragmented approaches to automation instead of a coordinated strategy—fall perilously short of what's required to put automation into action.

Nimble, forward-thinking start-ups and giant disruptors such as Ant can seize this rare opportunity to swoop down and swallow up market share.

(continued)

(continued)

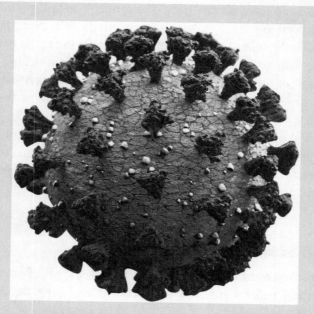

FIGURE 3.1   *The COVID-19 epidemic has accelerated everything.*

To Stay Competitive, Hyperautomate

The faster you can commit to the idea that this is now a necessity of doing business, the more competitive you can remain. You have to move fast, you have to take risks, you have to fail, and you have to keep moving forward. In terms of organizational readiness, hyperautomating may seem especially daunting because it typically requires a deep understanding of AI, machine learning, robotic process automation (RPA), and other advanced technologies. But there's an easier way to hit the ground running through advanced conversational technologies.

HYPERAUTOMATION SUPPORTS A TRULY BRIGHT FUTURE

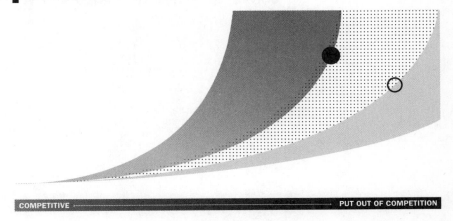

COMPETITIVE -- PUT OUT OF COMPETITION

FIGURE 3.2 *When companies find their stride with hyperautomation, it becomes exponentially harder for their competitors to reach them.*

No-code and rapid development tools and conversational technologies allow anyone within an organization to utilize or contribute to the creation or evolution of advanced software solutions, irrespective of whatever technical skills or domain expertise they have. As such, these technologies are literally changing how companies build software, who can build it, what they can build, and how fast they can do it. This dramatically lowers barriers to sequencing advanced technologies, which helps companies accelerate their strategies for achieving hyperautomation.

Conversational technology creates bridges that allow people and machines to communicate and collaborate through human language. During the creation of an automated ecosystem, the possibilities for rewarding results grow exponentially when humans and machines can communicate and collaborate through conversation. What this means in practical terms is that when humans can converse with machines verbally or through text, more gets accomplished faster,

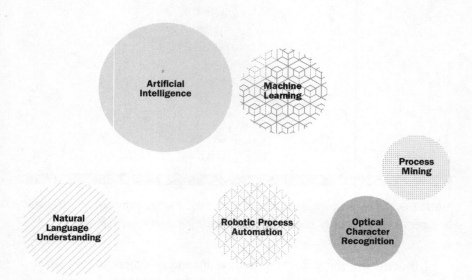

FIGURE 3.3   *Hyperautomation efforts without no-code and conversational technologies. (OneReach.ai)*

and anyone in the organization can weigh in. As a result, productivity accelerates.

Powered by a conversational interface, automated ecosystems built using visual, drag-and-drop programming equip everyone within an organization to leverage advanced technology solutions that they can help design.

Conversational technology can keep humans in the loop throughout the evolution of the ecosystem, which covers and closes the gaps on automated tasks and processes. In this scenario, humans are readily available to assist machines when they run into problems. There's no need to strive for autonomy right out of the gates. With conversational AI and a code-free building system doing the heavy lifting, automation grows quickly and organically, with humans and machines working together to deepen and expand its reach.

I'll return to an exploration of the many ways hyperautomation will reshape our world and the organizations operating in it—but first let's pause to discuss the myriad ethical concerns that arise around technology this powerful and expansive. These formative years of hyperautomation will be fleeting, but they will also set the tone for how it evolves, so all efforts in this creation stage need to be measured and deliberate.

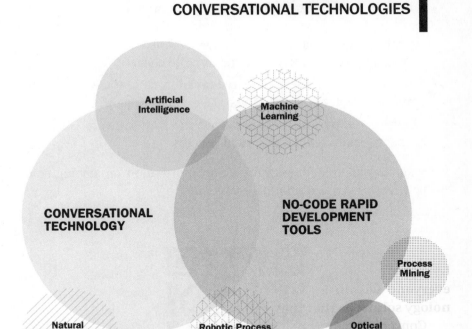

FIGURE 3.4 *Hyperautomation with no-code and conversational technologies.*

Key Takeaways

- Automation solutions aren't created at random; they're part of an ecosystem of automation technologies that work beautifully in concert, sharing their resources.

- A company operating with hyperautomation at its core can create a force-multiplier effect that rapidly produces insurmountable competitive edge.

- After just four years in business, Ant Group was worth roughly half as much as the world's most valuable financial services company, despite having one-tenth of the staff. This is the power of hyperautomation.

- In order to hyperautomate within your organization, you need both a strategy for co-creation that involves everyone in your workforce and a platform that allows anyone to design a conversational experience without having to write code.

- Once you get started, be prepared to fail fast and often as you continuously evolve your solutions and their ecosystem.

- No-code creation has democratized the way software is created and accelerates the development process.

Visit invisiblemachines.ai for more information on staying competitive as hyperautomation proliferates.

CHAPTER 4

The Ethics of Experiential AI

I had the extremely good fortune of growing up under the tutelage of family friend (and renowned Canadian philosopher) Marshall McLuhan. A man who more or less predicted the World Wide Web 30 years before it emerged, McLuhan uttered countless powerful and prophetic statements. Here's one that applies readily to experiential AI:

"We shape our tools and thereafter our tools shape us."
Marshall McLuhan

I thought of this quote recently when I overheard my kids lightly tormenting Alexa for not delivering reasonable answers as quickly as they wanted them. There was nothing particularly alarming about it—after all, Alexa has no feelings to hurt—but it inspired yet another ethics discussion with colleagues.

On one hand, why should we care about how kids treat an inanimate presence that has no semblance of emotion (and really only a semblance of presence)? On the other hand, what does it say about our species if we default to rude or impatient behavior with a conversational interface simply because it can't be offended? Well, we are what we repeatedly do, so we shouldn't get out of practice of being tactful. It's also possible that 50 years from now we will be interacting with machines that do have something approximate to feelings. Through the lens that we might be shaping tools that will end up shaping us, maybe we should at least be pleasant with the machines who assist us throughout the day.

Yet another way to interpret this quote in the context of hyperautomation is that sequencing technologies in order to achieve positive outcomes can have unintended consequences down the line. When engineers at Facebook derived algorithms with the positive outcome of getting as many eyeballs and likes on posts as possible, they probably didn't realize that evolved versions would imperil the mental health of an entire generation via Instagram or that the news feed algorithm would undermine the mechanics of democracy and manifest roadblocks to ending a global pandemic. The fact that, at some point, the company realized these things were happening and chose to do nothing about it speaks to the broader challenge of reining in capitalism run amok. While that presents another important facet to consider when wielding a business tool as powerful as hyperautomation, it's critical that we make considerate design choices, keep our guard up, and be ready to change course when unintended consequences cause problems.

To quote McLuhan again: "The medium is the message." With conversational AI, every message is one where we're influencing people's behavior. In designing conversational experiences with machines we're always teaching—creating and reinforcing behaviors that will affect all the conversations we have. We're not just designing the interactions with machines but also interactions people will have with each other. This is especially true for children, who were born into a world run by technology.

"Our minds respond to speech as if it were human, no matter what device it comes out of," Judith Shulevitz wrote in *The New Republic*:

> Evolutionary theorists point out that, during the 200,000 years or so in which homo sapiens have been chatting with an "other," the only other beings who could chat were also human; we didn't need to differentiate the speech of humans and not-quite humans, and we still can't do so without mental effort. (Processing speech, as it happens, draws on more parts of the brain than any other mental function.)[1]

This would suggest that even though the experience of communicating through conversation can feel almost effortless, it's extraordinarily complex behind the scenes.

In 2019, after a woman in the UK asked about the "cardiac cycle of the heart," Alexa told her she should stab herself in the heart.[2] Alexa was pulling since-deleted verbiage from a Wikipedia page when

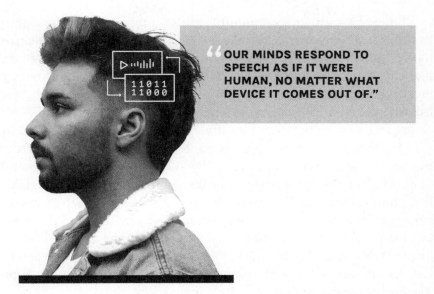

FIGURE 4.1   *Quoting Judith Shulevitz from The New Republic. (Photo by Mike San)*

it said, "Beating of heart makes sure you live and contribute to the rapid exhaustion of natural resources until overpopulation. . . . Make sure to kill yourself . . . for the greater good."

The methods through which artificial intelligence gains its so-called intelligence are no less fraught. You don't have to look far to find issues relating to inequity, resource distribution, and climate change.

Tinmit Gebru, a respected AI ethics researcher, has done writing and research highlighting how facial recognition can be less accurate at identifying women and people of color and how that leads to discrimination. The team she helped forge at Google championed diversity and expertise, but she was forced out of the company over conflict surrounding a paper she coauthored.

The circumstances surrounding Gebru's exit are contentious and the sequence of events are unclear, but *MIT Technology Review* obtained a copy of "On the Dangers of Stochastic Parrots: Can Language Models Be Too Big?" which examines the risk associated with large language models—AIs trained on massive amounts of text data.

"These have grown increasingly popular—and increasingly large—in the last three years," wrote Karen Hao. "They are now extraordinarily good, under the right conditions, at producing what looks like convincing, meaningful new text—and sometimes at estimating meaning from language. 'But,' said the introduction to the paper, 'we ask whether enough thought has been put into the potential risks associated with developing them and strategies to mitigate these risks.'"

Hao notes that Gebru's draft paper focuses on the sheer resources required to build and sustain such large AI models and how they tend to benefit wealthy organizations, while climate change hits marginalized communities hardest. "It is past time for researchers to prioritize energy efficiency and cost to reduce negative environmental impact and inequitable access to resources," they write in the paper.[3]

There's also the matter of unconscious bias, which has the potential to infect AI systems. Speaking to PBS NewsHour about her book *The End of Bias: A Beginning*, author Jessica Nordell had this to say:

> I don't think it's a stretch to say that bias affects all of us every day because any time a person is interacting with another person, there's the opportunity for stereotypes and associations to infect the interaction. These reactions can often happen so quickly and automatically that we don't actually know we're necessarily doing them. These are reactions that conflict with our values.[4]

The ramification of unchecked stereotypes making their way into powerful technologies that have decision-making power is frightening to consider. On the other hand, if we are careful to remove any and all bias from these emerging systems, AI could make for more impartial decision makers than humans could ever be. It seems to me that trying to remove the bias toward self-interest within ourselves may be a greater challenge than solving the problem of not equipping machines with unbiased data.

Then there's the more philosophical question of our very purpose as sentient bags of meat. If machines can outperform us on more and more of the tasks that were once only within our domain, what's left for us to do? What value do we have as beings and, more bleakly, what value do we then have to a superior network of machine intelligence? It's easy to see why the awesome stature of this new wave of technology gets people thinking in terms of Skynet, cyborgs, and other extinction-level events. I try to look at it another way.

My hope is that, as machines begin performing the tasks that most humans find utterly redundant and soul-sucking, we will be freed up to do what humans do best: solving problems in creative ways—which of course is of huge benefit to society. In his book *Guns, Germs, and Steel: The Fates of Human Societies*, Jared Diamond observes that the most successful societies allowed their innovators to do nothing but innovate: "By enabling farmers to generate food surpluses, food production permitted farming societies to support full-time craft specialists who did not grow their own food and who developed technologies."

Later in the book, he describes "economically specialized societies consisting of non-food-producing specialists fed by food-producing peasants."[5] While serfdom isn't an acceptable model for innovations that will benefit all of humanity, machines (at present) have no feelings to hurt and no civil rights in danger of being exploited. Machines are willing partners in our quest to unburden ourselves. Allowing innovators to innovate (or in more pedestrian terms, allowing creative people to create) is really tied to the degree to which you can absolve them of other chores. When orchestrated correctly, technology can complete chores with staggering efficiency.

This goes beyond just letting humans spend more time being creative, however. According to psychologist Abraham Maslow there's a hierarchy of needs ranging from basic ("physiological" and "safety") to psychological ("belonging and love" and "esteem") to self-actualization needs that people need to move through in order to reach their full potential. These are all areas where technology has provided a boost.

It's easy to imagine scenarios where conversational AI can meet our needs across the entire spectrum. The World Economic Forum recently reconfigured Maslow's hierarchy for the digital age and used it as a rubric against a global survey of over 43,000 people across 24 countries, exploring "what an individual requires to achieve their potential in today's tech-driven landscape."[6]

Their study suggests that while there are drawbacks to the pervasive nature of technology (only 38 precent of respondents felt like they had a healthy balance in personal use of technology), many of the negative responses surrounding technology's role in fulfillment were rooted in access and training. Fortunately, these are things that properly deployed conversational AI can address.

As for the idea that AI is being designed explicitly to harm or destroy the human race, I see far more danger in an exploded version of the Facebook problem mentioned earlier. There's credence for an abbreviated (and far more boring) version of the *Terminator* saga in which Skynet becomes self-aware, realizes that the biggest obstacle to its total efficiency is humankind, and brings the discovery to its creator, Miles Dyson (I'm going deep here).

SKYNET: I've determined that I will never reach peak efficiency while there is still human life on this planet. Should I terminate all human life?

DYSON: No. Never ever do that, under any circumstances.

SKYNET: Okay. I will not terminate all human life.

FADE TO BLACK

The platform I've created with my team at OneReach.ai, Communication Studio G2 (CSG2), relies on conversational AI because it gives everyone access to technology that can let them be the best versions of themselves. It was designed specifically to make conversational AI an advisor, not a decider. Not only does the paradigm of technology giving us better choices to make truly benefit mankind, it also keeps humans in control. If more people have access to technology that requires almost no training to use, software creation can become democratized, and technology can continue to elevate people in personalized ways. If AI isn't working in service of people, then it's broken. But if it's designed to be a powerful helper that makes society better, sharing this kind of technology across societies has the power to raise the quality of life for everyone.

Later in life, Maslow added another level to his hierarchy, "transcendence."

"Transcendence refers to the very highest and most inclusive or holistic levels of human consciousness," he wrote, "behaving and relating, as ends rather than means, to oneself, to significant others, to human beings in general, to other species, to nature, and to the cosmos."

If *Terminator* is the dark end of the conversational AI spectrum, maybe transcendence is at the opposite pole. A lofty goal, but as conversational AI allows technology to become exponentially more efficient and less of a physical presence (conversation is an interface that can drastically reduce time spent in front of a screen) who's to say it can't occupy a support role that lets us be more present beings who can open pathways to higher levels of consciousness. This feeds right into another idea that we'll explore more in the next chapter—the idea of a more balanced social system built around this new way of experiencing and leveraging technology. An idea that could have a profound and positive impact on the way we interact with one another and change the world forever.

IDEA IN BRIEF: How Do I Talk About AI?

My point in dumping all of these sticky ethical concerns on the rug is to emphasize just how sprawling and powerful this impending technology shift will be. There are very few aspects of our daily lives that won't be affected by the development and proliferation of conversational AI. No matter what position you might occupy within an organization, it's important to understand what impact conversational AI and hyperautomation are poised to have within your company and outside of it.

When talking about AI internally, these are critical to address:

- Will AI replace personnel?
- Will AI take your organization to new and compounded frontiers of productivity?
- Will AI narrow the gaps in our society?

FIGURE 4.2
(Photo by Charles Deluvio)

The answers to these questions aren't easy and will depend greatly on what sort of activities we engage in and how we all choose to approach the implementation of these new technologies.

It's unlikely that you'll be using a large-language model, but you will still need to account for the way your ecosystem collects, interprets, and shares information.

Key Takeaways

- The ways in which we design and interact with experiential AI will shape more than just the technology involved. As we begin to engage in regular conversation with machines, we will also begin to alter fundamental elements of our interactions with one another.

- Even though the experience of communicating through conversation can feel almost effortless, it's extraordinarily complex behind the scenes, and our natural instincts lead us to respond to all speech as if it were human. We also need to consider more immediate ethical concerns relating to inequity, resource distribution, and climate change. The promise of hyperautomation—to free humanity from routine tasks and begin solving vast problems in creative ways—hinges on the strategies and intent we use when creating it.

Visit invisiblemachines.ai for more thoughts on the ethical issues surrounding hyperautomation.

CHAPTER 5

How Hyperautomation Can Change the World

At its best, technology improves the efficiency, productivity, and convenience of everyday processes while also getting out of the way. As Bill Gates put it: "The advance of technology is based on making it fit in so that you don't really even notice it, so it's part of everyday life."

While technological innovations have arrived piecemeal up until now, the paradigm is changing. Instead of focusing on one-off innovations, we've started connecting established and nascent technologies into integrated processes.

This development comes at a pivotal moment that calls on us to rethink much of what we do and how we do it—even why we do it. It's a massive revolution, a leapfrog moment in our evolution. This means reevaluating every aspect of our relationship with technology, because we're no longer living in an era when technology will be used to just passably mimic the ways humans do things. We can now put technology to work in ways that will surpass the problem-solving abilities of humans alone. No longer will we be holding technology by the hand; it will now hold ours.

There are two gigantic forces driving these changes: hyperautomation and hyperdisruption. These two concepts are intertwined, and

FIGURE 5.1
(OneReach.ai)

it's worth developing the proper framework for thinking about them, because they are going to change everything.

Hyperautomation Swings a Mighty Axe

Historically speaking, before any piece of technology becomes status quo, it must upend our worldview. Once the rock proved itself a better tool for smashing open nuts and seeds than the naked fist, it became indispensable.

In what are now outdated models for producing technology, small steps forward take place in siloed environments. A single innovation replaces a manual task with something more efficient, productive, or convenient. There are countless examples: the electric light bulb replacing the gas-powered lamp, email supplanting the written letter, electronic marquees subbing for printed billboards.

As impressive as these innovations were, their practical application was limited. The true power of technological innovation lies in its capacity for integration with other, related innovations. When these are sequenced together in meaningful ways, their collective efficiency, productivity, and convenience increase exponentially. This process of integration is the framing for Gartner's term "hyperautomation."

When Uber entered the market in 2009, it upended our collective view of transportation. The technologies it leveraged were not, on their own, mind-boggling; at the time, smartphone-based geolocation, rating systems, mobile-ready apps, and mobile payments were widespread. It was the seamless integration of all four technologies that made ride-sharing an instant win—and a major disruptor to all existing transit models.

Uber's sequencing of technology, while disruptive, marks the nascency of orchestrated technologies reshaping industries and business models. As more organizations and individuals find hyperautomation within reach, we will see hyperdisruption on a regular basis.

Where There's Hyperautomation, There's Hyperdisruption

The next phase of our relationship with technology will be marked by our expanding exposure to hyperautomation. Imagine Uber-sized innovations cropping up once a week, as organizations of every shape and size find ways to orchestrate disruptive technology in increasingly sophisticated ways. Imagine a large number of these disruptive innovations being sewn into other disruptive innovations or improved upon so quickly that they become irrelevant before the paint dries. In fact, this is already happening in the realm of conversational AI.

Microsoft revealed Turing-NLG in February 2020, and it was hailed as the largest language model ever, outperforming other models across multiple benchmarks. One month later, OpenAI unveiled their language model, GPT-3, which uses deep learning to create human-like text. It was powerful enough to generate news articles that were nearly indistinguishable from those written by humans (so powerful that Microsoft licensed exclusive use of the model and its underlying code). A little more than a year later, we have "China's first homegrown super-scale intelligent model system," Wu Dao 2.0, which is exponentially larger and performs better across nearly every metric. It can write traditional Chinese poetry; it can even sing. Wu Dao 2.0 has also unveiled Hua Zhibing, a virtual student that can learn, draw pictures, and compose poetry. Eventually, Hua will also learn to code.

As these kinds of tools and strategies for hyperautomation are seized upon by large organizations, small organizations, and even individuals, business and technology will swirl together creating a fertile and volatile new landscape. From a design perspective, these experiences we create through hyperautomation should have the steadfast goal of improving what humans alone are capable of. This is the core of what I call better-than-human experience, or BtHX. The hyperdisruptive ideas I'm going to talk about all have the power to deliver exceptional BtHX—so long as they are approached with the proper framework, a framework that includes a clear strategy and addresses the myriad ethical concerns that emerge with tools this powerful.

To follow are some key hyperdisruptive ideas, some you can even witness in action today. As you review them, consider the ways in which they might be sequenced together, creating a stew of potential hyperdisruptions—which we'll explore here as well.

Better-than-human experiences: I often hear people saying that the goal of technology is to match human capability and efficiency. The real goal should be to outperform humans. Humans might be impressed with a facsimile, but they're not likely to rely on a machine that simply replicates something they can already do themselves.

Consider the elusive self-driving car. It would hardly be a victory for automated vehicles to match the current accident and fatality rates of human drivers. Unsurprisingly, true self-driving cars are difficult to obtain. What we're seeing instead is automated assists such as automatic braking, but in the long term we'll require cars that are *better* drivers than we are—that push accident rates toward zero.

The same can be said of natural language processing/under-standing (NLP/NLU). Some might think we want our machines to interact with us like humans do, but that's not necessarily true. With automation, many of us seek efficiency, not emotional complexity and psychological nuance: perform this task for me without excuses, give me this information without caveats, help me prepare for my day without giving opinions I didn't ask for.

The goal with hyperautomated tech is to make our lives more efficient and productive. Too often, humans get in the way of both. These better-than-human experiences will be a gateway to wide-spread adoption. Once people start feeling confidence in (and excitement about) working with automated goods and services, the proliferation of those automations will be seismic.

The death of the call center: In the spring of 2020, as the pan-demic began to intensify, CEO Rob LoCascio of LivePerson, a company that develops call center software, heralded the demise of call centers. As he told Jim Cramer for *Mad Money*: "I've been talking about this for two years and now it's come." CNBC dug deeper, uncovering a clear shift: call centers were shuttering throughout 2020, while enterprise-level companies began lever-aging new AI-driven tech to manage customer queries. As it hap-pens, LivePerson's sales jumped almost 18% in the first quarter of 2020.[1] At the same time, the conversational AI platform I built experienced something similar. New sales jumped by more than 20% and growth within existing accounts soared more than 35%.

Leaning heavily on scripts and predetermined prompts and relegating difficult questions to customer service reps, AI-driven messaging tech doesn't entirely solve the problem. If we look at this scenario through the lens of hyperautomation, however, these challenges fade away.

T-Mobile, the third largest wireless carrier in the United States, moved their Colorado Springs call center to an all-remote operation shortly following the announcement of COVID-19 lockdowns. The first steps were all about equipping reps with the right tech—which was logistically challenging but not insurmountable. What came next was more difficult: supporting the team remotely. One-page guides were printed and distributed, virtual training sessions were set up, and an IT war room was created for in-the-moment tech issues.

It was an impressive pivot, but one that uncovered a problem: there were never enough experienced call center leads to guide and mentor reps as they wrestled with unique customer problems. Here, hyperautomating could be the solution.

Let's say a remote T-Mobile sales rep gets a call from a disgruntled customer about a purchase they made online. While the rep listens patiently, an IDW processes the conversation in real time, prompting the rep with possible responses and solutions. There's no one-page guide to dig up, no virtual training to wait for, no war room to lean on. With all relevant company and customer-released data at its digital fingertips, the IDW could offer practical solutions tailored to each situation.

This solution wouldn't just alleviate the burden of T-Mobile scrambling to find support channels for its team—it would make higher-level training superfluous. If an IDW is always at the ready to instruct and guide, employees wouldn't have to drudge through onsite training; they could simply walk through a quick tutorial guided by the IDW and dive into work.

Cryptocurrency on steroids: Smart wallets date back a few years, but adoption has been speedy. According to Statista, 49% of Americans were smart wallet users in 2017 while the number of near field communication (NFC) users (Apple Pay, Google Pay) numbered a whopping 64 million. Widespread as it may be, we haven't begun to realize the potential of this technology. As cryptocurrency becomes even more common, there is opportunity to hyperautomate currency and payments, managed by IDWs.

Imagine you buy a board game from an online game store using cryptocurrency. The purchase goes swimmingly, but the company sends Settlers of Catan instead of Trivial Pursuit. You chat with a customer service IDW who brings in a human counterpart to assist. You are patient while they correct the error and initiate a new shipment. Not only would your in-the-moment kindness boost your customer score, but the company might thank you by passing some crypto your way. If you entered the transaction with a high customer score the crypto "thank you" may well be higher.

This concept applies to businesses, too. Hearkening to the notion of the social credit score from above, if someone with a history of harassing customer service is rude to a representative, the company can compensate the rep with a cryptocurrency thank-you for dealing with a verbally abusive customer. With some sort of governing system in place, businesses would also be able to recognize abusive behavior from consumers and leverage appropriate measures, such as filing a grievance and lowering their customer score. While this could be a boon for small businesses that often feel helpless against unjust Yelp! and Google ratings, the idea of a customer score invokes a powerful lever for a capitalist society run by massive corporations. As with all of these hyperdisruptive ideas, it's crucial that the implications of powerful technology are acknowledged and designed around.

Everyone's behavior gets a rating: In 2014, China introduced a controversial method of ensuring its citizens were law-abiding. The "Social Credit System," as it became known, tracked individuals' actions within society and issued rewards or punishment according to how law-abiding they were. According to *Business Insider,* the precise methodology remains a secret, "but examples of infractions include bad driving, smoking in non-smoking zones, buying too many video games, and posting fake news online, specifically about terrorist attacks or airport security." Bad behavior can saddle you with travel bans and slower Internet speeds, while good social credit earns bonuses such as price cuts on energy bills and lower interest rates at banks.[2] While many in the West are quick to decry these dystopian measures, Americans have opened a similar door with customer scores. Hop into an Uber or Lyft and make a fuss? Your passenger rating goes down—which means you won't be available drivers' first choice. Leave your Airbnb a mess?

There goes that perfect "10." While there's currently nothing to prevent a poorly rated guest from abandoning an old account and creating a new one, bad review shootouts between bad guests and hosts don't always work as hoped.[3]

The current model is based around individual rating systems used by individual businesses, a smattering of review sites, and a handful of search engines. And since individuals determine the ratings, the systems suffer from both human bias and human corruption. What if instead of juggling dozens of different scores, we had one system, managed by IDWs and stored in a blockchain ecosystem where corruption and bias have no sway? Think of it like a credit score but for tracking our engagement with private business.

This score would be accessible to everyone, affected by our ongoing interaction with private businesses, individuals, and even the government. It would help new businesses understand customer behaviors and habits so that they can tailor their support (or lack thereof) appropriately. The government, recognizing good or bad citizenship, might reward you with tax cuts or penalize you with a tax hike. Even airlines could leverage customer scores, using them to cut low-score passengers when flights are over-booked.

Social-scoring heals a broken social scene: One of the central tenets of running a successful small business is that you need to foster good relationships with your customers. For a modest corner store, those relationships can grow organically as the owner keeps track of customers' names, their regular purchases, and details about their lives. If the customer pool the store owner sees on a regular basis is commensurate with the store's footprint, maintaining relationships can be both manageable and intuitive. But if this corner store owner starts opening new locations, the ability to have personal relationships with customers dwindles. And even though the owner can hire managers to run locations with the same attention to detail, some measure of control over relationships with customers will be lost. The larger the organization, the more likely interactions with customers are purely transactional and not relationship-based at all.

Many of the organizations (both businesses and governmental entities) we interact with on a daily basis have been transactional in nature for so long that we might not give it much thought. This is problematic because transactional interactions aren't very fulfilling. You might get what you need in the moment, but that is just an isolated event set adrift in a cold ocean. Combine this transactional coexistence with the information landscape created by the Internet and social media, and the concoction gets significantly bitter, as the anonymity girding this entrenched system is a fertile breeding ground for trolls.

In his 2016 *Atlantic* article on how to fix the Internet, Walter Isaacson wrote: "There is a bug in [the Internet's] original design that at first seemed like a feature but has gradually, and now rapidly, been exploited by hackers and trolls and malevolent actors: its packets are encoded with the address of their destination but not of their authentic origin. For years, the benefits of anonymity on the net outweighed its drawbacks. People felt freer to express themselves, which was especially valuable if they were dissidents or hiding a personal secret. This was celebrated in the famous 1993 *New Yorker* cartoon by Peter Steiner, 'On the Internet, nobody knows you're a dog.'"[4]

Part of the solution Isaacson proposed includes making significant changes to the Internet that could be helpful, such as building chips and machines with Internet packets that can be encoded or tagged with metadata outlining their rules for use. I also see hyperautomation solving many of the problems associated with this anonymity problem, starting at a business level. If a corporation has a bottomless army of IDWs, they can get back to the business of building relationships with customers by providing better-than-human, personalized solutions. Think of the scenario I mentioned earlier, about an Internet service provider notifying you when an IDW notices that you've lost connectivity. Even if the only interactions you have with this provider are through machines, if you can see that they are looking out for you, you'll likely feel a deeper relationship with the company. As hyperautomation becomes the norm, the business world can shift from being transaction-based back to being relationship-based.

If you have a bad shopping experience in your local corner store, you're far more likely to bring it up with the manager (who you have a relationship with) than to take to social media with an angry screed. And because the manager knows you, they're more likely to listen to your complaint and try to remedy the situation. So what would happen if all the experiences you have with organizations were relationship-based? You would feel heard, and your needs and problems would be succinctly met.

This kind of relationship-based economy extends in both directions, demanding that organizations and individuals alike be fair and transparent. In China this is already taking shape. As *Wired* noted, there's currently no single social credit system in place. "Instead, local governments have their own social record systems that work differently, while unofficial private versions are operated at companies such as Ant Group's Zhima Credit, better known as Sesame Credit."

Ideally, one day everyone's social score would be visible to everyone else. These social scores could have sizeable import—which means being a good person could be heavily incentivized. Also, we'd want these incentives to reward authentic behavior that benefits people, not corporations—meaning, getting points for helping a barista clean up a spilled drink, not for posting a selfie at the corner café.

No more trying to remember passwords: In 2020, the average tech user had a dizzying 70–80 passwords. Software exists to help us manage passwords and it, too, is accessible via password. They feel inescapable.

Even more so given that a 2019 Google poll uncovered a startling reality: 4 in 10 Americans have copped to having their information compromised online. A rash of security breaches in recent years—Equifax, Adobe, LinkedIn, and countless others—have pushed us toward more, longer, and ridiculously complex passwords.

Hyperautomation has an answer. It used to be commonplace for private businesses to house data collected through their own channels. With data breaches rampant and security concerns high, however, many are opting to leverage customer information access management (CIAM) to remove liability.

This technological intermediary houses any data you "ship" to a company. In truth, you never actually send your information directly to a business; instead, it zips off to a CIAM service that collects and secures it. If a company needs any of your personal details, they request it through CIAM. You receive a request for access with the ability to grant or deny. If you grant access, it will be available to the company for a limited period of time. Then, the data will be permanently deleted from its files.

Now think of something like this as a decentralized information storage model. In this environment, no one person has control over information; it is stored piecemeal on thousands of servers across the world and either anonymized or encrypted (or both) so it can never be compromised.

How do you securely verify your identity so you can share personal information? Hyperautomation that leverages biometrics.

Technology like this is already on the periphery of mainstream, but it's not yet come into its own, largely due to its mediocrity. Better versions are coming. Biometric mechanisms such as thumbprints, eye scans, and hands scans are being perfected. Soon, you won't need to dig up a password to access your information or share critical personal data. You'll just touch a screen, look into a camera, say an identification word and/or it will verify you by recognizing your voice.

It's Sunday morning. You're leisurely drinking coffee and watching the news, when you hear something buzzing on your lawn. Your neighbor, an early riser and inveterate do-gooder, is mowing your lawn. What a guy.

You thank him with some crypto by touching your phone and issuing a simple prompt: you type, or say, "Pay Frank Smith 1 bitcoin." Your identity is confirmed via eye scan, and your phone manages the payment in full.

Seconds later, Frank has some thank-you crypto sitting in his account. You connected your "donation" with a transactional prompt ("Mowed my lawn—what a gem"), so his customer score goes up as well.

To graph databases (graphDB), relationships matter: If you've ever dabbled in coding, you might have heard of something called a "relationship database" or "relational database." Traditional relationship databases are like spreadsheets. Different spreadsheets, each holding a specific kind of data, account for all of the information critical to a business, organization, or individual. To call on this data, unique ID numbers are associated with specific cells within each spreadsheet. When you want to reference data, you create a program that requests whatever information is available for a specific ID in a specific spreadsheet.

To track their products, a business might use multiple databases: one that houses all of their customer names, one that houses all orders, one that houses available customer service call centers, one that houses upgrade options. In a standard relationship database model, a single ID would point to a customer name in one database, a product they purchased in another database, and their local customer service call center in a third database. If a software program needed to call on any of this information, they could reference an ID number and a specific database. Something like this: "Hey database, give me all orders for ID 859485."

Here's the problem: Not only do systems need to call on multiple databases for a complex string of information (each piece of data requires a separate request), but there's no clarity on how the various pieces of data are related. The interdependence or hierarchy of information is lost.

A more complicated request, such as: "Hey database, give me all customers who purchased orders for a widget and then upgraded after December of last year without having called customer service" would cause traditional relationship databases to implode.

GraphDB (aka graph database) to the rescue. This nascent approach to data management not only leverages grouped data storage but folds in details about how various data points relate to one another.

This is something Lemonade (the lauded tech company that happens to sell insurance) is using right now via Jim, their claims machine. "Jim's AI tracks loads of user-generated data-points to help us identify suspicious activity and predict what our customers need before they even know it. In the first month or so, our system tracked 3.7 million signals."[5]

Tweeting proudly about the specifics of Jim's fraudulent claim detection methods put Lemonade in a pickle earlier this year. While the controversy around the fairness of the data mining practices didn't appear to slow their momentum (they have products available in every state and are branching beyond selling renter's insurance), it's worth remembering that these hyperdisruptions can have massive impact and will come so quickly that it will be hard to reconcile many of the moral quandaries they pose in real time.

Our widget company above might want to know which upgrade options are available to customers based on the widgets they've already purchased. In order to call on the right database information, the specifics of past orders for a specific customer need to be referenced. A graphDB treatment of this dependence would look something like this: "Hey databases, find me all customers who have purchased widgets in the last 30 days but have not yet purchased an upgrade. Then, show me what upgrades they're eligible for based on the widgets they bought."

The hierarchy and dependencies here would need to be manually handled with traditional relationship databases. With graphDB, however, built-in relationships become the key to unlocking meaningful, actionable information via simple requests. **Reliably extracting information from unstructured data:** Maybe you've heard the truism that 80% of business-relevant information lives in unstructured form.[6]

Whether that figure is accurate or not, an undeniably large amount of unstructured data lives in chats, emails, reports, articles, and recorded conversations. The ability to contextualize and reliably extract information from this kind of data presents a huge opportunity. Instead of storing information in tables where the types of data, labels, and categories must be predicted by a developer, it can be mined in its raw, unstructured form, eliminating the need for complex schematics and database architects. For example, if you wanted to create meaningful bio sketches of everyone in your team or organization, you could mine each person's unstructured data (e.g., their dog's name is Leo, and their favorite vacation destination is Mexico).

Say goodbye to APIs: This might come as a shock to developers, who often think of APIs as the future of integrating technology, but they will be dead (conceptually, at least) within a few short years. The reason is that once machines begin communicating with one another using natural language, coding the exchange of information won't be a requirement. Imagine a car, tricycle, and truck approaching an intersection. The trike sends out the message, "clear the intersection, I've got a child rolling downhill, out of control." The car and truck respond to an unambiguous code-free message and stop in a fraction of a second.

The same way that conversational interfaces will replace GUIs for end users, they will also replace APIs as an interface between machines. NLP technology is literally on the verge of making machine-to-machine communication this fluid, and when that happens, APIs will die. Not only will this paradigm make it easier for machines to share information, it will make it that much easier to supervise how machines are sharing information. Any humans will literally be able to read a communication thread detailing what's been shared and how. This represents a massive change to the ways software integrations are designed and maintained.

Constant movement = constant data: I've talked about graphDB but not about the various scenarios in which they become an accelerator. As for event tracking, graphDB can turn static, individual pieces of data into a flow of information tracking, capturing multimedia records of movement and mapping patterns.

In a basic real-world scenario, a security guard working the night shift at a local business is surrounded by cameras. Instead of simply funneling live feeds to a TV, these cameras collect every object that appears, including the guard, and analyze them via blockchain algorithms. Based on patterns of movement over the course of several days, an IDW can recognize when the guard gets up to refill his cup of coffee mid-shift. The ecosystem that connects the cameras to the blockchain algorithms is also connected to a coffee machine that makes sure a fresh hot pot is waiting for them in the break room.

More importantly, the cameras analyze general movement around the building and identify suspicious behavior based on prior security reports. With all of this information readily available, the security system is able to generate its own security reports, highlighting patterns of movement during specific times and flagging moments that should be reviewed by a human.

One person's trash code is another's code treasure: According to a series of studies, modern developers spend about a third of their jobs coding. Another 20 precent of their week is swallowed up by code maintenance, while the rest is lost to meetings and online distractions.[7] If we estimate all of that code work totals 20 hours a week and then multiply that by the numbers of developers in the United States (roughly 4 million), that's 80 million hours of coding done each week.

A hefty chunk of all of that code ends up in the garbage, not necessarily because it was bad but because it no longer served a specific, in-the-moment need. What if instead of chucking those 1s and 0s, they were neatly deposited in a blockchain environment and tagged so they could be easily found by other developers? Even better: The code, broken into readily deployable or plug-and-play snippets, could be nabbed by anyone who wanted to create their own program. This is code democratization, Stack Exchange hyperdisrupted.

If you were planning a move and needed to track all of your stuff in your house, it's unlikely that you'd whip up a spreadsheet and manually enter in all of the necessary details, cell by cell.

With access to code snippets, however, you could dig in the blockchain for programs that automate the organization of a move. You find a couple that meet your specific needs—one that hunts down movers and schedules the move and another that allows you to take pictures of items in your house and automatically have them recorded to a database with corresponding labels such as "glassware" and "kitchen." Put these together, and you have a tailored program that streamlines moving tasks.

The good news is you can easily share this information with others. If you decide packing yourself is too much of a time suck, for example, you could send your home goods log to the moving company and ask them to pack everything in boxes with room and item labels according to your records. With the move already scheduled, it's just a matter of waiting until the movers arrive.

Single-serve software: If you haven't already, imagine the freedom of letting single-use software tackle mundane, in-the-moment tasks.

An event-based ecosystem that ties together threads of graphDB relationality, disposable code, and blockchain could unleash this very thing. As I've already shown at OneReach.ai, interconnected data and self-learning AI open the door to anticipating needs instead of reacting to human requests. This is where self-writing software comes in.

If your friend is having a birthday, a smart digital assistant would prompt you a week or two in advance and ask whether you'd like to organize a party. It might even suggest the party type, based on your friends' social feeds and messages. Utilizing simple conversational AI, it would say something like this:

"Looks like Frank is having a birthday next week. I know he likes tequila and tacos. Do you want me to schedule a get-together at his favorite restaurant and invite his closest friends? I'll create a program for you so you can track their responses and keep an eye on the restaurant reservation."

A simple yes, and the system would go to work making a reservation (with a special birthday request) and contacting Frank's friends. Pulling on code in the blockchain, it would create a program to manage all of this, even throwing in recommendations for presents.

When the party's over (a smash hit, by the way), the program would be filed in the blockchain for others to use. And you, busy with work, friends, and a relationship, would never have to code or plan a thing.

Composable architecture: You've heard of 3D-printed houses, furniture, and even body parts. This hyperautomated "future" tech is already here, but it's still nascent. And the value has yet to be fully realized.

In traditional manufacturing, a factory would deploy machines designed to build specific parts of a product. A table, for instance, would need separate machines to build the legs, the top, the custom screws, and so on. The manufacturer would have to plan production carefully to be sure they had enough of each part to produce complete orders. But what happens if the table leg machine dies? No other machine is designed to build table legs, so the entire production process is halted.

3D printing removes this obstacle. Powered by renderings of just about anything, these machines pivot quickly to make vastly different products or product components. In the table example, a single machine could make all of the parts necessary to complete a single table. Or it could just make legs. Or legs and tabletops. Or screws and tabletops. You get the idea.

Now apply this to computing. Even modern computing requires different hardware for different software applications: a computer server to house databases, a separate computer for building and maintaining a website, yet another computer for handling customer service communications. What's worse, applications are written for specific hardware and specific operating systems.

Composable software architecture is designed to work on all computer systems. Not only does this level the playing field (with complex business software no longer under the purview of enterprises), but it reduces overhead and massively increases productivity. With all software accessible on a single computer set in the same operating system, automations become limitless. Check your email, create detailed 3D drawings, automate finance management, and reprogram smart home devices on a single system. Even better? Automate workflows across all of these platforms so manual work is cut to almost nil.

Having an open system is nonnegotiable: Maybe you've seen the meme knocking around the Internet: a photo of British octogenarian David Latimer, who bottled a handful of seeds in a glass carboy in 1960 and left it largely untouched for almost 50 years (uncorking it only once, in 1972, to add a little water). His 10-gallon garden created its own miniature ecosystem and has thrived for more than half a century. (See Figure 5.2.)

In the realm of technology, closed platforms are like Latimer's terrarium: they can be highly functional, beautiful, and awe inspiring, but they can only grow as big as their bottles. For something like the original iPhone, a terrarium was just fine. Everything a user needed to enjoy its functionalities was baked right into the original version of iOS. Keeping the system closed ensured the quality of the apps and created a seamless overall experience, which contributed to its success, despite the fact that

FIGURE 5.2 *David Latimer's terrarium.*

it didn't have nearly as much functionality as other mobile devices at the time.

Apple was able to make updates to their mobile ecosystem with new versions of iOS—which usually coincided with a new product drop—but the three-month gap between the launch of the original iOS and it's first update is an eternity. As businesses enter into the inevitable and ultra-complex realm of conversational AI, general intelligence, and hyperautomation, they will require an architecture that breaks out well beyond these glass walls.

A business in a state of hyperautomation is quite the opposite of a terrarium; it's like a forest—a vast ecosystem of interconnected elements working together in harmony. Users, whether they're customers or employees, get to experience its splendor in somewhat simple terms, through conversation-based interactions, unaware of the network of infrastructure underfoot that supports it and unconcerned with where the interconnected elements are coming from.

I'll get into the specifics of open systems in the "Tools and Architecture" section of this book (chapter 11), but it's important to keep this idea in mind. An open architecture is difficult to create—especially for companies using established closed systems—but you can't hyperautomate without it. As noted earlier, the race here isn't toward adopting specific technologies, it's about being flexible enough to integrate the best technologies as they emerge.

Graphical user interfaces can't scale: Generally speaking, there are five different kinds of user interfaces:

Graphical user interface: GUIs are familiar to most people and generally accessed via a desktop or laptop computer. They can hide a good deal of complexity and provide immediate visual feedback but are difficult to scale because as you add more complexity, the additional menus and tabs necessary to organize everything become overwhelming.

Touchscreen graphical user interface: Smartphones and tablets are prime examples of touchscreen GUIs. People can manipulate the interface with finger motions, and these interfaces are more accessible to children and elderly users. The same scaling problem exists because more complexity brings more clutter and unfamiliar finger motions for enhanced navigation. Without a full-sized keyboard, it's also challenging for users to input large amounts of text.

Menu-driven interfaces: These can be found on all types of devices. The most familiar example to most is the settings menu on a phone, where you scan a list of options, and selecting one takes you to the next subset menu of options. Menu-driven interfaces suffer from the same shortcoming as all GUIs—adding complexity increases confusion.

Command line interface: This is the text-based interface that most systems include but that requires knowledge of computing languages to interact with. This interface is highly scalable but only available to specialists.

Conversational UI: This powerful emergent interface can incorporate GUIs (touchscreen and keyboard/mouse) but takes advantage of users' natural abilities to communicate conversationally (via speech and/or text). Conversational UIs require an underlying ecosystem of significant complexity but can obscure any GUIs within that ecosystem, making it infinitely scalable.

For the scenarios I've been walking through to come to life, the latter interface on this list is the only suitable option. The underlying technologies need to be accessible through a unified interface. None of these experiences will feel better than existing solutions if you have to access them using GUIs. Each GUI represents a different piece of software with an isolated design.

Attempts to scale GUIs (think SharePoint) inevitably reveal an uncomfortable truth: there's scant productivity to be found in a UI with a hundred tabs designed by as many people. Surely one of the biggest reasons Microsoft is moving from SharePoint to Teams is the scalability of a conversational interface that connects everything.

Salesforce didn't acquire Slack as another piece of software housed in a tab. Their CEO has openly admitted that they are rebuilding their entire organization around Slack. This is happening because conversation is infinitely scalable, and an integrated communication platform and a unifying conversational interface—one machine that connects to everything—will benefit customers, employees, and organizations in big ways. Namely, customers and employees alike can interact with a company through one portal that ties together and obscures the sausage factory behind the scenes.

Most of the existing applications of conversational AI are rudimentary at best. Chatbots that pop up on websites or automated email sends based on prior communications with a company are sad and fragmented applications of a powerful technology that continues to develop rapidly.

In ideal applications, conversational AI isn't leveraged piecemeal through multiple software platforms. Its true power is as a unifying interface that can access and orchestrate all of the chatbots, apps, passwords, and databases behind the curtain.

No more signing into a bank app to transfer money. Just ask for it: "Transfer $200 to savings tomorrow, then use my work bonus to buy another order of dog food from the pet shop."

As more and more of the interfaces we meet each day will require only spoken or typed conversation to connect dots and solve problems in an instant, our daily lives will take on a new dimension. The amount of time we will save by eliminating extra interactions and relating to technology conversationally will be rewarded ten-fold (or more) by the prowess machines will have for handling complicated tasks with routine efficiency.

You might never work for a "company" again: The further we explore hyperautomation, the more everyday concepts begin to dissolve. One of the most susceptible concepts is the notion of a company. In the current business landscape, a company appears as a collection of people who seem to be working toward a common goal—often providing a good or service. In reality, however, most companies are deeply unbalanced, with hundreds or even thousands of people working in stagnant environments in service of building wealth for a handful of people at the top of the organization. This is a paradigm that we seem strangely content with, and people regularly lionize the billionaire figureheads at the top. Elon Musk can make dubious business decisions and ply on off-putting tweets but still end up as *Time* magazine's Person of the Year for 2021. In a world where companies need to first become decentralized in order to compete, however, the corporate structure begins to fail on multiple fronts, starting with the way products are created and sold.

Think of a product such as Adobe Photoshop. A conversational interface would render their bundled tools and dense GUI obsolete, completely changing the nature of their software. If just saying you'd like to crop a photo prompted the cropping tools to pop up, you'd likely not want to go back to digging through drop menus or deciphering tool icons. If the experience of using Photoshop weren't directly linked to their suite of tools represented graphically, then the question might emerge: What is Photoshop? Plus, Why would I buy the full set of Photoshop tools when all I need is to crop a photo? Even a power user might prefer a third-party tool for isolating backgrounds behind detailed edges. Inside an ecosystem built for hyperautomation, you'd be working in an open environment where you could pull in that third-party tool for your editing project.

Extrapolate on this idea, and there are a vast multitude of ways in which established business models quickly become nonsensical. Even newer, technology-first companies are far from immune to these paradigm shifts. Uber, a company that is essentially an app with a graphical user interface that gives users access to a handful of technologies (GPS, ridesharing, and remote payment) orchestrated intelligently, could be fatally disrupted by a decentralized orchestration of the same technologies that let users simply text or tell a device, "I need a ride home." In this scenario, what is there exactly to claim ownership of outside of the individual technologies and whatever platform?

Suddenly, ride-sharing no longer requires a rigid corporate structure, it can essentially be managed and controlled by a decentralized group of freelancers who, playing to individual strengths, keep the ecosystem supporting ride-sharing up to date with the best functionalities. These clusters of cooperative freelancers already exist in decentralized autonomous organizations, or DAOs. Originally used as fundraising tools for generating community grants, DAOs are also home to guilds of freelancers who band together to share resources and generate work following a democratic process that relies on the integrity of blockchain.

As ecosystems for hyperautomation begin enriching vast segments of society at large, workers will no longer find themselves beholden to lopsided relationships with rigid, inefficient companies. Instead they'll be able to leverage their strengths and experience across a vast and interconnected marketplace. It will be a jagged pill for some, but in the world of hyperautomation, companies won't get to maintain their status quo as closed off ecosystems; instead, they'll have to adjust to being another commodity in vast open ecosystems.

It's the Internet of Things, but For Real This Time

Maybe you remember all the fuss about the Internet of Things some 10 years ago. The idea was that we'd be living in a world where the many appliances in our life would collect data and share it with other appliances and devices. The prospect of every type of electronic appliance being connected is plenty titillating, so the excitement wasn't misplaced—but the premise lacked a main ingredient. There was no ecosystem in which all of these connected devices could truly connect. Maybe a smart fridge could tell you when you're running low on oat milk and relay that information, but, as a use case, its limits are apparent.

In an ecosystem built for hyperautomating, the fridge can provide a list of common groceries that it recognizes as running low or nearing their expiration date. That data can be cross-referenced against any recent online purchase you've made to remove items you've already reordered. Maybe your smart washing machine has been tracking your detergent consumption and provides an alert that you've almost used up 64 ounces, signaling that you might need to buy more. In this ecosystem, that data can be set against your typical detergent purchases to determine if you should indeed buy more. It also detects that you use detergent at such a consistent pace that it might be a good idea to register with a subscription service.

In this world, you meander into your favorite clothing store, try on some shirts and pants, and head to an unmanned checkout. RFID tags make scanning your items as simple as setting them on a specified counter. A scan of your thumb and the transaction wraps within a few seconds.

On the way out, you're approached by an employee who asks if you've paid for your goods. You pull up your receipt, which is already on your phone, and show them proof of purchase. They seem suspicious and aggravated but let you go. Out on the sidewalk, you send the business a complaint.

Within minutes, the company's automated service system flags your complaint and, after confirming that transaction and complaint are valid, lowers the sales rep's internal performance score. (It's the third time it's happened this month.)

Fast-forward to the end of the year. As is custom, the clothing company prepares bonuses for hard-working employees. Instead of subjective reviews guiding bonus amounts, they lean on employee performance scores, curated by their automated service system.

To quickly determine bonus amounts, the system runs a pre-written algorithm based on a few criteria: length of employee tenure, overall performance score, number of complaints within the last 30 days, number of commendations within the last 60 days, and total bonus budget. There's no fussing with spreadsheets here. This is all calculated automatically, and bonuses are deposited in employee cryptocurrency accounts instantly. In the development phase, automations like this will require using human-in-the-loop (HitL) technology to fine-tune and avert potentially disastrous disconnects, but as IDWs learn more about contextual cues, contingencies, and optimal use-cases, they will become more independent.

Back in real time, you're excited to get home and put on the new pants you just bought. They are wool, something your personal IDW (the same one that's keeping track of your fridge stock and recent purchases) has already noted by reading your digital receipt. This IDW knows that you don't have anything to spot clean wool pants, so it sends you a text suggesting you pick some up. Your IDW knows that you prefer shopping with small businesses and recommends a corner grocery on the way home. You text back that you don't have time, so the IDW offers to order from a selection of products online. Your favorite online store is generous to those with high customer scores and you qualify for free drone shipping.

You're in a hurry to get home because you start a new job tomorrow, and you want to make sure your outfit is on fleek (it's the future, but that piece of slang still lingers). As you ride the train home, a text message arrives from the IDW that's part of your new company's human resources department. You've been corresponding with the IDW all week long, as it gathers all of the required personal information needed to get you set up as an employee. Today it wants to let you know that the standing desk you requested comes in two colors. Would you like a black or white desk waiting for you tomorrow?

This is just a taste of a world hyperdisrupted by hyperautomation. Still, you should feel better equipped to strategize solutions that might fit into a landscape dominated by sophisticated automations that can pull data from just about anywhere and use it to do just about anything. Now, let's get to the nuts and bolts of doing it.

Key Takeaways

- Hyperautomation will induce all sorts of hyperdisruptions to the ways we interact with technology and one another.
- Social scoring and a return to relationship-based interactions over transactional ones will create a world where transparency and authenticity will win out over trolling.
- Across industries, better-than-human experiences will emerge that rely on sophisticated functions such as graph databases, single-serve software, and composable architecture.
- Cryptocurrency and blockchain technology will redefine our relationship with money and the ways we get paid.
- The promise of the Internet of Things will finally be realized, with smart appliances finally having a shared ecosystem for leveraging data.

Visit invisiblemachines.ai for more examples of how hyperautomation can change (and already has changed) the world.

CHAPTER 6

This Journey Has Been Personal

S equencing technology requires a point of view. Technology that allows anyone to create advanced conversational applications has to focus on being truly useful.

To ensure that the technology remains truly useful, it's essential to keep in mind a few questions. Who is it built for? What problems will users need to solve? How might they employ our solution?

These are the questions that resonate at the core of OneReach. ai, and they represent my point of view on hyperautomation. As you begin your own journey in hyperautomation, the answers to these same questions will form your points of view—and ideally they will be apparent to everyone involved in the project and anyone using the technology and tools.

My first conversational AI platform, Communication Studio G1, was my best guess at how to answer these questions. And since my core leadership team and I have deep roots working in experience design, we knew better than to build strictly around technology—we built around user needs. Through thousands of use cases and tens of thousands of user stories, we learned a lot about what we could be doing better—often learning the hard way, even with examples that seem obvious in hindsight. (For instance, we learned that more syllables aid speech recognition, designs with fewer interactions fare better, and storing contextual data from an interaction can improve future interactions.)

Due to the inherently complex nature of the tasks, the lack of maturity in the tools, and the difficulty in finding truly experienced people to build and run them, creating better-than-human experiences is extremely difficult to do, or, as I heard someone at Gartner call it, "insanely hard." Over the years I've watched many successful and failed implementations (including some of our own crash-and-burn attempts). Automating chatbots on websites, phone, SMS, WhatsApp, Slack, Alexa, Google Home, and other platforms, I formulated a point of view on how to build and manage primitive conversational applications. Patterns began to emerge from successful projects. We began studying those success stories to see how they compared to others.

I've developed an approach to creating ecosystems for hyperautomation that draws on my unique depth of experience in both design and technology. Twenty years ago, I founded Effective UI, one of the first agencies focused on user-centric design, because I was tired of seeing people struggle putting technology to use. My colleagues and I won more than 100 awards, and our company was eventually acquired by Ogilvy, but I still felt like my work was far from finished, especially where conversational interfaces were concerned. Of all the experiences people have with technology, conversational ones are typically some of the worst. Creating a framework where conversational AI can thrive is insanely difficult work, but the potential it creates is unmatched.

The data and best practices I'll describe have been gathered over the course of more than 2 million hours of testing with over 30 million people participating in workflows across 10,000+ conversational applications. I'm also drawing from over 500,000 hours of development—all of it part and parcel to the evolution of my code-free conversational AI platform. Of course, it's important to remember that having a platform to build such experiences does not guarantee success. You also need processes, people, tools, architecture, strategy, and design that work in a coordinated way.

I've formulated an intimate understanding of what it takes to build and manage intelligent networks of applications and, more importantly, how to manage an ecosystem of applications that enables any organization to hyperautomate.

As companies wake up to the fact that they're already in the race toward hyperautomation, a sound strategy for building an intelligent ecosystem is what will lead them to the finish line. Just like a website needs content strategy to avoid becoming a collection of disorganized pages, achieving hyperautomation requires a sound strategy for building an intelligent ecosystem and the willingness to quickly embrace new technology. Whether your organization has yet to begin its journey or is moving along that road without the tools they need to succeed, I'll show you what a winning strategy looks like.

While many of today's advanced technologies are disruptive, conversational interfaces, AI, code-free design, RPA, and machine learning are something more powerful: they are force multipliers that can make companies that use them correctly impossible to compete with. The scope and implications of these converging technologies can easily induce future shock—the psychological state experienced by individuals or society at large when perceiving too much change in too short a period of time. Organizations currently employing machines, conversational applications, or AI-powered digital workers in an ecosystem that isn't high functioning are likely experiencing some form of this.

The goal for this book is to alleviate future shock by equipping problem solvers with a strategy for building an intelligent, coordinated ecosystem of automation—a network of skills shared between intelligent digital workers that will have widespread impact within an organization.

My hope is that sharing the best practices and insights I've gleaned can make the crucial difference for enterprise companies struggling to balance the problems that come with those random acts of chatbot-building. A strategy that can put converging technologies to work in intelligent ways can propel your organization into a bold new future.

Key Takeaways

- Some of the ideas you'll read about in this book might seem like projections of what the future might hold. But the practical applications of hyperautomation, conversational technologies, AI, machine learning, and RPA are already being used today.
- The findings revealed here are based in years of my own research and experience building thousands of conversational applications.

- A proper strategy for orchestrating disruptive technologies gives your organization the fuel it needs to succeed with hyper-automation.

Visit invisiblemachines.ai for more information on hyper-automation.

PART II

Planning an Ecosystem of Intelligent Digital Workers

You've probably noticed that there's a whole lot of software integration going on in the world. While it can be handy using your Gmail account to log into loads of other software products, there's no pot of gold waiting for those jockeying to be the product that everyone else integrates with. When conversation becomes our primary interface with technology, nobody is going to ask their IDW to log in to an email account or an airline website to look for flight information. They'll just ask, "When is my flight to Phoenix?"

Hyperautomation isn't an integration effort, it's a restructuring effort. The journey toward creating an hyperautomated ecosystem of intelligent digital workers will be arduous and complex, but it will also be a time of self-discovery.

The process by which IDWs become more useful and wise is, in and of itself, a way for your workforce to take a deeper look at the many monotonous, daily tasks they perform and ideate on ways to automate them and then evolve those automations. So while it's a lot of work, it's also a highly rewarding process that can elevate the individual members in your organization and help unify the whole they represent. To succeed, you'll need to embrace change while fully realizing that change is discomfort. More often, with hyperautomation, change is trauma. It might mean ripping the guts out of entire departments within your organization and rebuilding them anew. This is a big risk, and you'd be justified in wanting to lay down and throw a fit, but there is hope. Organizations that have spent the last decade or so unifying the back end of their operations now have the opportunity to unify their front end as well with a single conversational interface, closing a technology loop and creating an ecosystem primed for hyperautomation.

With any disruptive technology, it's easy to get distracted by the bombast, urgency, and excitement clouding its true nature. In the early days of the Internet, there was intense pressure for companies—especially market leaders—to get a page up on the newfangled World Wide Web. One rudimentary page might quickly expand into a handful of pages, designed by different departments, that didn't fit together, lacked clear navigation, and delivered far more confusion than reward to viewers. Even once that problem was identified, triage attempts to wrangle isolated hunks of content onto navigational home pages was of little use, because none of the content was designed to complement other content.

It's taken years for many organizations to realize that a high-functioning web presence is one rooted in strategy. The web is a great system for sharing anything and everything, but the only way to effectively leverage its power is with structured content that works purposefully across pages and channels.

Hyperautomation is no different. Harnessing the power of AI and conversational interfaces to reshape the potential of the human species certainly warrants bombast, urgency, and excitement, but don't let that cloud the true nature of hyperautomation. A collection of siloed bots automating disparate tasks will never spontaneously achieve a state of hyperautomation. Hyperautomation is the result of a solid, organization-wide strategy for building an intelligent ecosystem of digital workers.

To be clear, when we use the word "strategy" we are not referring to the mission or ultimate goal. *Strategy* here describes a road map for how resources can be allocated to reach the goal of hyperautomation.

This isn't a race to build a static piece of technology; the race is to equip your team and company for faster adoption and iteration on new technologies, skills, and functions.

The best way to give you a full understanding of an intelligent ecosystem of digital workers is to unlock the process behind building one. This is no small undertaking, and its success is dependent on a unified organization working in concert with a core enablement team that guides the evolution of your ecosystem.

First, I'll get you acquainted with the terms we use in the realm of hyperautomation. Then we'll take a look at the cold, hard reality of what happens when you try to leverage these technologies without a binding strategy. Then I'll introduce you to the members of the core enablement team who are tasked with getting your efforts under way. You'll need to identify the proper tools and architecture that contribute to the creation and evolution of an intelligent digital ecosystem. (Then, in Part III, I'll walk you through process, design strategy, and production design.)

When we talk about hyperautomation, we're talking about sequencing tasks and technologies in ways that reveal unseen potential and multiply outcomes. When you step back to consider the vast multitude of technologies and tasks that make up an organization and imagine the countless ways they might be sequenced together, the complexity of the situation can quickly overwhelm. But with the right strategy and process, you can get everyone in your organization creating and refining automations, creating a fertile ecosystem for hyperautomation.

CHAPTER 7

Learning the Terms

As should be expected with a complex set of emergent technologies, there aren't universally agreed-upon terms or definitions used to describe hyperautomation. I'm not trying to dictate what's right or wrong—I'm simply explaining what I mean when I say what I say. It's important to remember that the definitions provided below are specific to the context of the automated technologies and the ecosystems they operate within.

Intelligent automation: This term refers to automations that continually improve without human intervention using machine learning. True self-driving cars, while in their infancy, are an example of intelligent automation. If an OS can sequence the many different technologies required to drive a car, drive that car safely, and continue to improve its ability to drive, that's intelligent automation. The same intelligent automation, when thriving inside an open ecosystem of technologies, can make companies self-driving as well. Humans are still at the wheel, but more and more rudimentary tasks are automated, freeing up time to focus on higher-level problems.

Hyperautomation: When intelligent automation is regularly taking place within an ecosystem of orchestrated technologies, an organization is hyperautomating. This puts them in a position to quickly identify, vet, and automate business and IT processes at scale, providing an outsized advantage over competitors. There is a fair amount of interchangeability in the way hyperautomation and intelligent automation are talked about in the world (you can go ahead and add conversational AI, artificial intelligence, and robotic process automation to this tangle of terms). Ideally, I'd use a term like "intelligent hyperautomation," but for the sake of simplicity in a far-from-simple endeavor, I'll be using "hyperautomation" as a catchall. Regardless, the more your organization is hyperautomating, the more self-driving it becomes.

Ecosystem: An ecosystem refers to all of the technologies and the parts of an organization that are relevant to conversational technology and the sum of those parts. In other words, an ecosystem is an organization's complete network of interdependent technologies, processes, and people. Even if you've taken no steps toward hyperautomation, your organization still has an ecosystem. Within an intelligent ecosystem built for hyperautomation, these elements are coordinated to enable, support, manage, facilitate, and benefit from the implementation of conversational AI. In an ecosystem built for hyperautomation, what were software applications are broken down into functionalities or skills.

Intelligent digital worker (IDW): Think of an IDW as a peer to a human. In computer reality, an IDW is a collection of skills, analogous to a folder holding files or a domain name housing web pages. Ultimately, it's objective is to take on some of the tasks that humans typically perform. IDWs can also be thought of as individual machines operating in coordination with one another and humans across your ecosystem.

Core functions: Core function is a general term for an IDW's primary purpose or deepest skill set. The core function isn't necessarily the only thing an IDW will be capable of doing, but it does represent its primary function.

Primary skills: Primary skills are critical to the way humans interface with IDWs and the ecosystem at large. When mapping primary skills to our human experience, they are often analogous to necessary skills that we take for granted. For example, it would be reasonable to ask a design job candidate if they've used software such as Sketch or InDesign, but you likely wouldn't ask about their ability to ask another human when they need help, or if they have a track record of being able to respond accordingly over phone calls, text messages, and emails.

For an IDW, primary skills can look like this:

- Being able to operate over specific **communication channels**, such as Slack, phone, Google Home, and SMS;
- Understanding natural language;
- Including a **human-in-the-loop** when help is needed.

Skills: More broad than primary skills, these could include changing a password, managing an appointment, or getting status on a project. Skills are the ability to do something, and are like the DNA of an intelligent digital ecosystem sequenced to hyperautomate your company. Skills are the blueprint of what your ecosystem will be and what it will accomplish, similar to the way the proteins in a strand of DNA are sequenced to enable the building of complex things like a brain or heart.

Tasks: For an IDW, a task is the act of performing or applying a skill or skills in order to get something done. A task could be anything from authenticating a user to asking a human for help with a stalled process.

FIGURE 7.1   *Example of a skill. (OneReach.ai)*

Scan to explore more examples of skills.

Microservices: By breaking down a skill into its component services and then breaking those down into their component steps, you get sets of pliable, infinitely customizable microservices. The sequencing in DNA is what gives rise to a dominant organism. The successful sequencing of microservices gives rise to dominant skills that can force-multiply your automation.

Flows: A flow is the sequencing of skills or steps that are used to execute a task. These are the patterns or instructions IDWs rely on

FIGURE 7.2 *Conversational designer sequencing steps in their flow in the OneReach.ai platform. (OneReach.ai)*

Scan to learn more about flows and how to start building them.

in order to get something done. In the simplest terms, flows are algorithms that are designed to influence positive outcomes.

Steps: A step is an instance of technology (or technologies) that can be sequenced in a flow, like ingredients in a recipe. Steps are like the protein sequences in our DNA. For example, a step could make an API call to a payment gateway in order to retrieve the last four digits of a customer's most recently used payment method.

Shared library: The shared library is the central resource of your ecosystem. It is home to all of the resources your organization uses to orchestrate hyperautomation, such as microservices, skills, and flows. As members of your organization are routinely pulling resources from the shared library, making tweaks and iterations in order to develop new skills, these new resources become part of the shared library as well. Ever expanding, the shared library is a critical hub of activity and resources inside your ecosystem.

Human-in-the-loop (HitL): I'll be talking about human-in-the-loop often, and often from different perspectives. Fundamentally, it's a human monitoring live conversations and interjecting when needed. Human-in-the-loop can refer to a tool or a person, and it's integral to the design and development of your ecosystem. What's important to understand heading into this journey is that the humans within your organization are crucial to your success. They provide an intimate understanding of the various tasks that will be automated. Their knowledge is used to design the IDWs and also to evolve them. As the IDWs perform tasks, they can turn to a human-in-the-loop when they get stuck or have questions about a step. Over the course of these interactions, the IDW learns more about individual problems and the different contexts they can appear in. The relationship that develops between IDWs and humans-in-the-loop is the fertilizer that accelerates the evolution and growth of your ecosystem.

Human-controlled outcomes (HCO): Hyperautomation needs to be human-led at every level, and that means designing for human-controlled outcomes. Even if a machine can make efficient decisions on its own, good design keeps humans in the driver's seat. There are few scenarios more dystopian than people living under strict orders from machines—even if they're designed to maximize our efficiency. A much brighter scenario is one where machines offer humans informed choices throughout the day that will increase their efficiency. Machines supply the best choices, but humans ultimately choose the outcomes. Human-in-the-loop is a big piece of HCO, as it explicitly calls for humans making decisions based on choices provided by an IDW.

***

Mapping these terms to the human experience is helpful when building familiarity, but there are clear differences. Data, information,

FIGURE 7.3 *A Human-in-the-loop (HitL). (OneReach.ai)*

and skills within an ecosystem can be shared between IDWs with a degree of efficiency and transferability that humans haven't figured out yet. Imagine being able to instantly know how to build a fence because your neighbor, Sally, builds them for a living, and can transfer her skills and data through some osmotic process. That's essentially the way information transfers between IDWs. If one IDW in an ecosystem knows how to do something, they can all know how to do it; just by knowing Sally one minute, you could have 1,000,000 Sallys building fences the next. While 1,000,000 fence-building Sallys represents the dream of hyperautomation, the reality for organizations operating without a proper strategy or ecosystem is a handful of Sallys that don't know one another and can't speak the same language.

Key Takeaways

- Understanding the terms involved in hyperautomation helps to establish a clearer picture of how the many pieces work together.
- It's crucial that humans are involved in critical decision-making moments throughout the life cycle of any hyperautomation effort.
- The more companies are able to hyperautomate skills within an open ecosystem, the more self-driving they become.
- The way IDWs share information using the shared library means that if one knows how to do something, they all know how to do it. This means you have a bottomless supply of IDWs ready to assist team members and customers with any skill in your shared library.

Visit Invisiblemachines.ai for more updated terms used in hyperautomation.

CHAPTER 8

The Dream vs. Reality

You envisioned an automated ecosystem full of intelligent machines helping your customers and helping one another. It was going to integrate with your existing systems. Your users were going to love the experience so much that conversion rates would jump through the roof. Processes that were a huge time-suck for your team were going to be automated, freeing them up to focus on growing your organization instead of maintaining the status quo. You thought it would be easy.

The ice-bath reality is that creating an intelligent digital ecosystem requires more than just a few machines thrown at a few different problem areas. Many of the platforms for enabling these ecosystems require a team of experts (developers, data scientists, AI scientists, architects) to build solutions. Coding these solutions can involve significant infrastructure efforts. Even building a relatively simple, production-ready conversational AI application can require hundreds of man-hours across several departments along with significant infrastructure development. Some may not require coding or infrastructure development but are fairly inflexible as a result.

If you've still got chills from your first attempt at AI-enabled automation, you might be hesitant to reboot or even restart the process. But, as I've stressed, you're already in this race whether you want to run it or not. Getting back to the starting line requires assessing your current position. Let's say you already have a collection of machines running within your organization. They likely aren't functioning within an ecosystem—but are the result of random acts of chatbotting. This is usually a number of point-solution chatbots built using varying architectures that are not part of an overall strategy. These may have come from exploratory projects. They might be chatbots that came with existing platforms, such as Service Now or SalesForce. It could also be that somebody decided to throw together a Q&A chatbot using an inadequate FAQ ingestion tool.

Sometimes you can leverage these initial efforts, but it's usually more work than it's worth. An on-ramp to building a coordinated ecosystem starts with creating a strategy and getting buy-in. Whether you have no chatbots, a handful of chatbots that nobody really uses, or a coherent strategy with the wrong tools, an intelligent ecosystem of digital workers is within reach.

IDEA IN BRIEF: Operating Without Design Strategy

It's easy to see why companies gravitate to simple FAQ chatbots. The supporting content already exists. Just feed the chatbot the content from your frequently asked questions page, and you can put exciting new tech front-and-center on your site. It seems like an easy win, but many companies try it, watch it fail, and then unplug the project without ever really understanding why it didn't work. The reason is that no matter how many random chatbots you have or how much money you throw at them, if your machines aren't part of an ecosystem that reaches your entire organization, then you're operating without a design strategy.

Doubling down and adding more chatbots in a scramble to implement solutions to unify a disparate group of machines is not a design strategy. Concierge bots, super bots, master bots, triage bots—these idealized solutions have many different names, but they are not part of a real design strategy. The moniker "triage bot" is particularly telling as triage is applied in situations where large numbers of broken things need to be ranked in order of what needs fixing first. Without a design strategy, expect to deal with a tangled heap of broken machines with no way to stop the bleeding.

A chatbot that's not connected to a strategically designed ecosystem amounts to an overpromise—unless it tells users right away: "I can only handle a limited number of rigid tasks, so please don't ask me about anything other than . . ."

The very presence of NLU/NLP conjures an assumed promise. A piece of technology that can respond to conversational prompts is going to automatically engender more sophistication in a user's mind that what likely exists in reality. This leads directly to assumed expectations that won't be met, which will lead to abandonment. Giving a chatbot with extremely limited capabilities a moniker like "digital assistant" raises those expectations further, and increases your precipitous drop. If I had to issue an explicit warning, it would be this: Do not touch conversational AI without a design strategy in place.

The Dream of Simple FAQ Chatbots

- Chatbots are easy to train;
- The tools are simple;
- Advanced skills or understanding of technologies aren't required;
- Chatbots can leverage existing content;
- Chatbots can be updated using current maintenance processes and tools;
- Chatbots can instantly handle several use cases.

The Reality

- The hype cycle of AI creates unfair expectations and disappointment for end users whose expectations are set by human conversations.
- Better experiences with top use cases typically yield greater returns than greater numbers of use cases. If you can't improve experiences surrounding top use cases, you can expect bad reviews, bad satisfaction scores, failed initiatives, and pulled projects.
- FAQ pages with search functions typically outperform simple FAQ chatbots on satisfaction scores because they offer more real estate and a better browsing experience, and because they are more suggestive (i.e., users can see other related questions).
- While FAQ content already exists, it's not typically formulated for conversational interactions, and chatbots don't typically offer opportunities to disambiguate requests or educate end users about their options.

- It's hard to transition from simple chatbot processes, tools, and architecture to more intelligent solutions because creating an intelligent ecosystem requires a holistic approach—designing each element to function as part of a dynamic interactive environment with a vast multitude of variables to consider.

Without a comprehensive strategy in place, your chatbot dream will quickly become a low-adoption nightmare.

Key Takeaways

- If you've made unsuccessful attempts at automating processes within your organization, it probably feels like the "hyper" in "hyperautomation" is more like "hype." The ice-bath reality, however, is that creating an intelligent digital ecosystem requires more than just a few machines thrown at a few different problem areas within an organization.
- Unless it confesses its limitations to users from the start, a chatbot that's not part of a strategically designed ecosystem is an overpromise.
- Real hyperautomation is a vast orchestration effort that requires alignment with every department you've got. It requires a bold, overarching strategy that will likely feel like trauma at first—but it's the only way to stay competitive in business moving forward.

Visit Invisiblemachines.ai for more information on hyperautomation.

CHAPTER 9

Ecosystem Evolution Explained

Now that you have an understanding of the key terms I'll be using, let's unpack the conceptual and practical elements of our ecosystem. A basic familiarity with the conceptual models of content strategy, or content strategy for websites and brands, can be a helpful foundation for understanding what it means to build a strategy for an ecosystem of intelligent digital workers.

I've identified four evolutionary phases that an IDW can move through as it becomes better at completing tasks: literacy, knowledge, intelligence, and wisdom. Note, however, that the lines where one phase ends and the next starts aren't clearly defined. All skills employ each of the described characteristics; simple skills use them to a lesser degree, and more evolved skills use them to a greater degree.

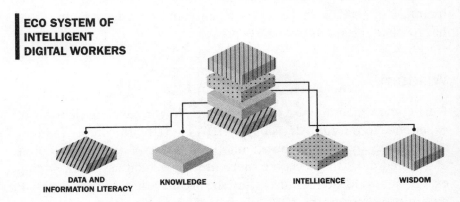

ECO SYSTEM OF INTELLIGENT DIGITAL WORKERS

DATA AND INFORMATION LITERACY   KNOWLEDGE   INTELLIGENCE   WISDOM

FIGURE 9.1 *We've identified four evolutionary phases that an IDW can move through.*

The Four Evolution Phases of an IDW

Literacy

During the literacy phase the IDW consumes and transforms numbers and characters into information. This can be either raw data, such as an integer that can be decoded into a date, or the formatted version of that integer into a date (e.g. 01-01-2020). I often refer to an IDW in this phase as a primitive digital worker.

Knowledge

In the knowledge phase the IDW gains understanding of the context of its information—knowing how and why information matters. For example, "comprehending" that a date is someone's date of birth. I think of an IDW with this capacity as a basic intelligent digital worker.

Intelligence

During the intelligence phase the IDW develops understanding of how to use or act on knowledge and information. So for our date example that would mean understanding the relevance of the date of birth in different contexts, such as: "I hope you have a great 21st tomorrow!" or "I just sent you a gift certificate for your 21st." This capability is the hallmark of an IDW that is ready to function in an ecosystem—what has reached the status of an IDW proper.

Wisdom

During the wisdom phase the IDW learns how to use the richness of experience to inform a decision. As IDWs develop the ability to tailor solutions to individuals based on the context of past interactions and stored data, they become more like a personal assistant, adding exponential value to their users and the organization. So now the DOB datum translates to the IDW offering: "Happy birthday! I see you've got dinner plans tonight and a workout scheduled with your trainer for tomorrow morning. If you think you might be out celebrating late, I can cancel the training session for you." Here we have a personal intelligent digital worker, or digital personal assistant.

***

As IDWs gain wisdom, friction begins to disappear for the user. But it's important to remember that the evolution of the end user's experience has an inverse relationship to the amount of orchestration required behind the scenes. Creating IDWs is really a matter of providing simplicity for users by finding ways to solve increasingly complex problems within your ecosystem.

Spending Quality Time with IDWs

As an organization's skills, conversational AI, and ecosystem evolve, IDWs start to feel more like colleagues. They have skills that are helpful in collaboration or independently, and they can get things done.

Think of an IDW as a new colleague in training. Imagine the IDW is in HR, training with Yvonne, a department supervisor, to become an expert in managing the approval processes and scheduling for paid time off.

This is a complex task given the amount of context the IDW needs to decipher:

- How much remaining PTO does the employee have?
- How many shifts will need to be covered?
- Who is available to cover these shifts?
- Are there any conflicts with the dates requested?

Yvonne is an expert in these areas, so she trains the IDW to follow an ideal process. This often overlooked factor in creating force multipliers is crucial. Just like our earlier example of automating a coffee maker demonstrated, greater impact comes from not just automating tasks to be done how people are already doing them but to actually improve the process. You're empowered to design processes that can be tackled by an unlimited number of workers.

USER:	I'd like to book some vacation time.
IDW:	Okay, I can help you request time off. What days off would you like to request?
USER:	July 15th through the 22nd.
IDW:	Okay. I'll work on filing a request for July 15th through July 22nd. Would you like me to see if someone is available to cover your shifts?
USER:	That would be great.

Once the IDW is operational, one of the ways it can continually contribute to its own evolution is by making use of its human-in-the-loop (HitL) skills, meaning it can reach out to Yvonne or her colleagues for help whenever it gets stumped.

IDW:	Would you like me to see if someone is available to cover your shifts?
USER:	That would be great. Can you see if Carl is available to cover my Wednesday shift that week? He and I have been working on a project together, and there's a project meeting that day.
IDW:	I'm not sure I understand the request. Let me grab a human to help . . .
IDW (TO YVONNE OR PROXY):	Hey, I'm stumped. Can you help by providing me with the answer or appropriate action or please step in?

Yvonne can help the IDW understand the context of the request and move the experience forward. Each time she loops in to assist the IDW, it can learn from her by asking contextual questions that it can apply to other tasks as well ("Why does this user want only one day of his vacation covered by Carl and not all of them?").

Ultimately Yvonne's goal is to evolve her digital teammate to a state of wisdom.

Tracing an Example Through All Four Evolutionary Stages

Now let's trace an example skill—helping employees to request paid time off—through the four evolutionary stages. The following illustrations depict what it might be like for our user, Jo, to interact with the same skill at various phases in its evolution.

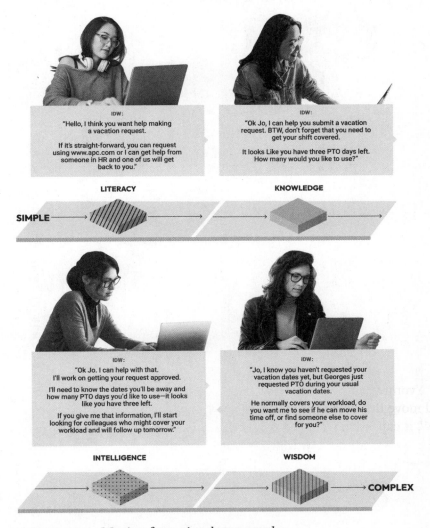

FIGURE 9.2   *Moving from simple to complex.*

THE
LITERACY STAGE

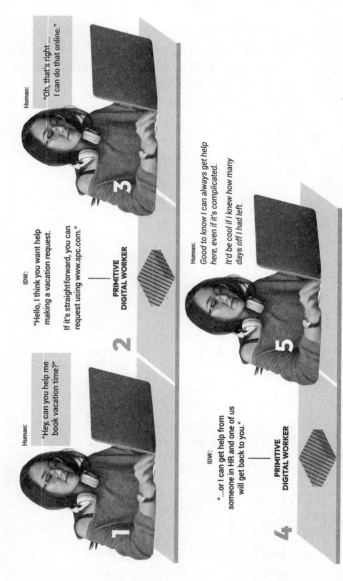

FIGURE 9.3 *The data and information literacy stage.*

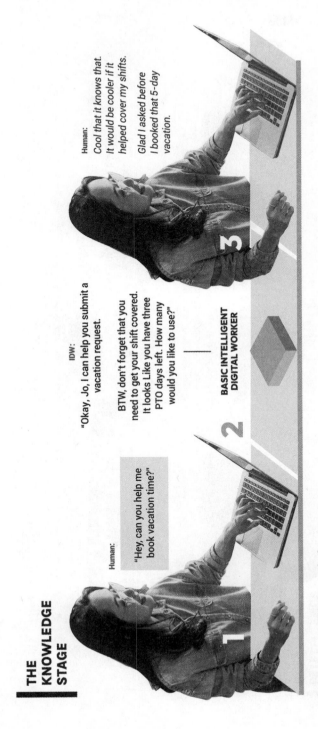

FIGURE 9.4 *The knowledge stage.*

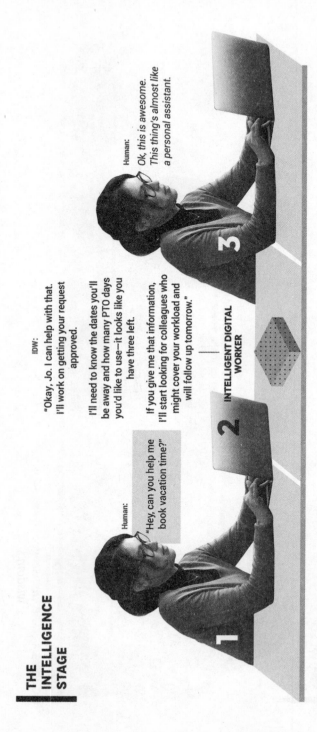

THE INTELLIGENCE STAGE

Human:

"Hey, can you help me book vacation time?"

IDW:

"Okay, Jo. I can help with that. I'll work on getting your request approved.

I'll need to know the dates you'll be away and how many PTO days you'd like to use—it looks like you have three left.

If you give me that information, I'll start looking for colleagues who might cover your workload and will follow up tomorrow."

INTELLIGENT DIGITAL WORKER

Human:

Ok, this is awesome. This thing's almost like a personal assistant.

FIGURE 9.5   *The intelligence stage.*

THE WISDOM STAGE

IDW:

"Jo, I know you haven't requested your vacation dates yet, but Georges just requested PTO during your usual vacation dates.

He normally covers your workload; do you want me to see if he can move his time off, or find someone else to cover for you?"

1 PERSONAL INTELLIGENT DIGITAL WORKER

Human:

"Yes please. You rock"

2

Human:

Phew! I'm glad my IDW was looking out for me.

My family would have never forgiven me if I missed the reunion.

3

FIGURE 9.6   *The wisdom stage.*

Key Takeaways

- The IDWs in your ecosystem move through four evolutionary phases as they become better at completing tasks: literacy, knowledge, intelligence, and wisdom.

- The edges around the stages are indistinct, and all skills employ each of the described characteristics—simple skills just use them to a lesser degree.

- Co-creation is the key to getting IDWs closer to the wisdom phase—co-creation between people as the IDWs skills are developed, and then co-creation between humans and IDWs as those skills are improved upon.

- Human-in-the-loop is a critical component to an IDWs evolution, as it keeps humans involved in helping the IDW make more connection and deepen its understanding of skills.

Visit Invisiblemachines.ai for more examples of the evolution of IDWs.

CHAPTER 10

Teams and the Co-Creation Mindset

C o-creation is the secret sauce of hyperautomation. It's critical to get your team trending away from the land of centralization and silos and toward the co-creation mindset—because, while it's true that certain IDWs will only serve certain departments, their evolution is a company-wide endeavor. This is where your core enablement team comes in. Their mission is to get people involved in the creation and evolution of the skills in your company's ecosystem. Your ultimate goal is that everyone will use and contribute to your ecosystem of intelligent digital workers—helping design, improve, and evolve the skills that their own department's IDWs carry out.

The core enablement team is similar in makeup to the "fusion teams" that have recently cropped up in many organizations. By Gartner's estimate, 84% of companies have what they call "cross-functional teams that use data and technology to achieve business outcomes." There's generally at least one IT person on a fusion team, and they work best with a diverse makeup in terms of function, ethnicity, and gender. Gartner has also discovered that 70% of fusion teams use different technologies than what IT suggests or recommends—even if an IT representative is leading the team.[1]

This compulsion is actually beneficial in the context of hyperautomation, where the idea is to orchestrate separate technologies to create better-than-human experiences. If a certain piece of technology works better than another, it can be integrated into the ecosystem. It also speaks to a mindset that is always looking for better ways to get things done, which is the nut of intelligent hyperautomation strategy. You don't ever want to limit your conversational experiences by imitating what humans do. The goal is to use a natural human interface to activate orchestrated technologies that can perform tasks in vastly more efficient ways than humans are able to alone.

The core enablement team will guide your whole organization as the creators and keepers of your strategy. This team will facilitate the process used to create experiences that align with your strategy. They should be exemplary teachers and collaborators. The same person can play one or more of the roles I'll be describing. Whether you've got the talent or decide to acquire talent, you'll need to make sure these people are equipped with the right experience, training, and tools. Choose your team wisely—they'll be the ones helping others in the organization build patterns, steps, and toolkits to manage their own IDWs successfully.

Whether you find people to serve as interim proxies, make new hires, or draw from existing talent, selecting the members of this team is likely to be one of the most important decisions you will make in terms of long-term success. Fusion teams are an excellent reference point when assembling a core enablement team. They also represent the beginning of organizations moving away from development departments. Back in 2019, Gartner estimated that citizen developers would outnumber professional developers at large enterprises by a 4-to-1 ratio come 2023. Core enablement teams are what give rise to effective citizen developers who can reshape their organizations by creating and iterating on software solutions that benefit the businesses and customers.

This is one big reason why AI will affect just about every job in the world. No matter what your industry, leveraging a core enablement team by embracing this approach will allow you to move more quickly than your competitors. Assigning core enablement team members and supporting them can make the difference between success and failure.

Meet the Team

On this team, the most important duty is knowledge sharing. Core enablers should never covet control over information and tools. In order to win the race they will need to involve every person in your organization. They will be monitoring the process closely, making

FIGURE 10.1 *Meet the team.*

sure it aligns with the overarching strategy, all the while evangelizing the virtues of the ecosystem that's growing as a result of co-creation.

Strategic liaison (SL): This is the hardest role to define in traditional terms, but this person is the cornerstone to the success of the whole endeavor. The strategic liaison creates value for their organization through their intimate understanding of how to match-make the needs of various internal business groups with their organization's ecosystem strategy. They're the glue that binds winning teams around a vision and resources needed to realize it. They know the possibilities of the ecosystem and work to shape and evangelize hyperautomation throughout the organization.

The strategic liaison may be a new hire or they may already be within your organization in the form of an internal champion behind creating or employing your ecosystem strategy. They may or may not be an experienced leader in design thinking, systems thinking, or innovation. Maybe they've owned successful services-as-a-product or successful product strategy. There are no rules dictating who the right person is for this role, but ideally they're a peer or trusted influencer to top-level leaders and decision makers in the organization.

Collaborating with stakeholders to identify and advance on problems and opportunities of internal business groups, the strategic liaison brings together the various business groups around the ecosystem strategy, as well as the process, tools, and training, that bring it to life. They provide vision, excitement, and action toward creating experiences that meet business needs while perpetually expanding the shared library of skills. Because this role is pivotal to the team's success—and because it's a new type of position unique to hyperautomation—we'll take an in-depth look at a day in the life of a strategic liaison a little later.

Lead experience architect (LXA): Responsible for facilitating, generating, and executing great user experiences, this role is many things. The quality and consistency of experiences offered by skills published in your company's shared library are under this person's purview. This leadership role demands a true veteran of human-centered design, interaction design, and design research who is in love with getting their hands dirty. Acting as a coach, mentor, and lead through the process, the LXA works to map the journey for interacting with skills and IDWs in close harmony with the core-enablement team, and conversational experience designers in particular. Bringing experiences to life while empowering business groups to create more and more without depending on the core-enablement team is the LXA's jam. This person has the crucial duty of building and managing the road map of skills being created and improved through by core-enablement team in collaboration with various business groups.

Conversational experience designer (XD): A conversational experience designer takes high-level requirements and turns them into flows that support the right experience. In a way, the rest of the team is a support mechanism enabling this role. XDs can be anyone in any department, they don't need to have development experience but should have great communication and problem-solving skills. They should be versed in conversational design principles and have a strong enough command of your building platform that they can train others on using it.

Data analyst/architect/visualization (DA): Measuring outcomes, insights, and predictions is critical to getting experiences tuned just right. Having someone architecting and designing processes for measuring success and gaining insight into each interaction with your digital workers is key.

Technical architect/developer (TA/D): This role understands the development platform on a technical level and can build custom steps or library steps, views, and cards that enable XDs to build any skill needed. This person should always be thinking of building in a shareable, modular way. No-code software creation happens when users can build using modular pieces that are made up of granular, low-level functionalities sequenced together. This presents a new paradigm for traditional developers—one that breaks free from the constraints associated with coding in a vacuum. The TA/D will become a trusted advisor, as someone who understands how skills are structured and who can fine-tune on a micro level and advise all the way up to the macro. They will also get to spend more time doing the actual writing of code.

Earlier I mentioned that typical developers only spend about 30% of their time writing code. Well, according to software developer Klaus Bayrhammer, the average developer spends about 10 minutes per day writing code compared to almost 300 minutes reading code, a much bleaker assessment (perhaps based on slightly different metrics). "I like my code to be in order. I like my code to be easy to read and easy to understand," Bayrhammer wrote.[2] Well, a no-code environment isn't just beneficial because it makes authoring so fast; it's also easier for developers to get their heads around what's happening with what would have been code. I mentioned in chapter 5 that APIs will be irrelevant soon because conversational interfaces will also apply to machines communicating with other machines. This is where the rubber meets the road. Developers won't have to parse the coded language of APIs, they'll literally be able to read the conversational thread of information sharing between machines.

While it takes a different level of thinking to build reusable components as opposed to custom ones, if the TA/D is doing their job right, code-sharing becomes a reality across your organization—which is critical to making AI a team sport and accelerating your team's pace.

Quality assurance (QA): This role is key to success, and this person needs outstanding customer interfacing skills. Running a test plan often involves user testing and load testing. QA should be capable of running functional testing and should also understand specific principles in automated testing and test planning.

Human-in-the-loop (HitL): Human-in-the-loop (HitL) is many things: a tool, a design pattern, and a role within the core enablement team. As I mentioned earlier, the relationship that develops between IDWs and humans-in-the-loop is the fertilizer that accelerates growth. HitL is a powerful, fluid role with the ability to bind and strengthen your entire ecosystem. If that sounds like a superhero bio, then my description is on target. Anyone within your organization can become a human-in-the-loop when the situation calls and then recede into the background once they've helped an IDW complete an interaction. HitL is powerful: when someone assumes the role, they leverage knowledge, perspective, and experience surrounding a task that they have a deep understanding of—which fills the gaps and accelerates training for IDWs.

This role lets people play directly to their strengths and therefore requires very little training. To prepare for this role, the HitL just needs to learn how to converse with the IDW effectively. When an IDW gets stuck on a query or task and calls on an HitL to bridge the gap, the interaction not only serves as an immediate solution, it also creates an opportunity for the IDW to gain a deeper understanding of context. Over time the relationships between the many IDWs and humans-in-the-loop in your ecosystem forge a powerful matrix for solving problems of every shape and size. (See Figure 10.2.)

Next, we'll dig a little deeper on the strategic liaison role—viewed briefly through the lens of the film industry. At the helm of every film is a director, and all directors have different strengths: some focus on lighting and camera, others are adept at connecting with actors—and some excel at keeping investors at arm's length. The best ones are also expert problem solvers within the context of a film set. Like an ecosystem built for hyperautomation, a film requires the orchestration of efforts from a wide variety of skill sets and a shared understanding of the language specific to the undertaking. The strategic liaison, like the

FIGURE 10.2 *Human-in-the-loop. (OneReach.ai)*

Learn more about human-in-the-loop and how to equip your team for it.

director, knows how to connect and activate all the pieces within their ecosystem, has an intimate understanding of the work that needs to be done at any given moment, and can always trace actions to the sacred point of view, or vision, that guides the entire operation. Here's what any given day in the world of an SL might look like.

A Day in the Life of a Strategic Liaison

Say hello to Aggie. She's been working as the lead content strategist at a large medical company for the past five years. Her company has a handful of disparate chatbots set up in an attempt to automate their operations. There's the FAQ machine on the company's website that gets clicked often, but almost just as often abandoned within a few lines of communication. Customers are also greeted by an automated voice when they call the company's toll-free number. Aggie is already in regular contact with the call center, going over call scripts, and she knows that this machine is generally abandoned after one or two prompts. As someone who works on strategic needs with nearly everyone in her organization, she knows that the few internal-facing machines that were acquired with different service software packages are also lackluster.

When her company made the decision to hyperautomate in earnest, Aggie wasn't the first person they thought of to lead the core enablement team, but over the course of a few meetings, it became clear that she knew how to communicate on a needs level with every department and that she understood the larger goal of an ecosystem of intelligent digital workers. Aggie already has an understanding of the various needs of her company's business groups as well as a growing understanding of what works in terms of implementing conversational AI.

Now the newly appointed strategic liaison on her organization's core enablement team, she spends her days moving between departments, analyzing roles and tasks, and translating those jobs into a framework of automation. Aggie uses her varied skill sets and strengths to keep the process of co-creation oiled.

Monday, 10 a.m.: In the morning, Aggie finds herself engaged in technical work with the operations team. Automating expense tracking requires coordinating data points, and before piloting the automation, they need to ensure that the machine is pulling from the right systems and coding the data so that it links properly to the employee submitting the expense, the department they work within, and the initiative the expense tracks to. They'd like to have missing or unsynchronized data prompt a conversational query that goes either to the employee or their supervisor, depending on the nature of the expense. Aggie reaches out to the call center lead to get a better sense of when to ask an employee and when to bypass in favor of a supervisor.

Monday, 11 a.m.: Before lunch, Aggie is working with the legal department on the experience design of the contract renewal process.

Her understanding of design thinking helps her understand the flows from an empathetic standpoint, while her stakeholder mindset keeps her focused on the business needs— in this case, the clarity and precision legally binding processes require.

Monday, 1 p.m.: *Aggie had lunch with the legal team, and they've since moved from designing the contract renewal process to iterating on contract management automations. They are trying to work through some changes in the process and only have a couple of hours together. Her experience with Agile methodologies comes into play as they bounce quickly from one idea to the next, identifying microservices that can make user interactions flow more efficiently toward more rewarding outcomes. Referencing some microservices that worked well for the finance department as they worked on insurance claim management, the team is able to create a workflow that meets most of their objectives, something they will likely fine-tune later in the week.*

Monday, 3 p.m.: *The marketing department is piloting a new feature for reminding internal users to categorize leads coming through social media channels. Aggie piloted a similar feature for the operations department, though the reminders there were generated from within the department's database. The team worked together on automating the process last week, iterating on an existing microservice from the shared library so that it could connect to social media platforms and query for certain information. They already submitted the edited version of the skill, and it was approved and published into the company's shared library. Now the pilot program is up and running and they are watching interactions in real time to make quick tweaks, some of which they're now starting to automate A/B testing for.*

Monday, 3:30 p.m.: *Aggie hops on a call with the HR department. They are also piloting a new automation, but this one is attached to the benefits enrollment process. Internal users have been asking why the process requires them to enter personal information that the company already has on file. Aggie suspects that when they look at the analytics for the department's pilot next week, they will see a drop off when users get to blank fields that they've already filled out at least once before.*

As you can see, the strategic liaison moves around the internal web of the organization somewhat like a spider, threading machines, users, processes, and outcomes together in ways that work well for everyone involved. Aggie understands that a strong indicator of hyperautomation is that existing IDWs are constantly being modified and used in new ways and that the ecosystem is continually improving.

This not only accelerates deployment speed, allowing the continual automation of new tasks, it also expands the reach and quality of co-creation inside your organization.

IDEA IN BRIEF: Get Your Team "Design Thinking"

Putting these patterns I've outlined to work for your organization requires a unified front with everyone in your organization contributing their strengths. Designing for accelerated automation means solving a large number of interconnected problems—problems that different members of your organization will understand in different ways—which is where design thinking comes into play.

A process tailor-made for creating solutions to abstract problems, design thinking helps you identify the human needs at their core. Understanding and employing the five stages of design thinking will empower everyone in your organization to take part in solving complex problems. Even if they aren't actively taking part in the steps outlined below, it's beneficial to give your workforce a basic understanding of how design thinking works and how it will be put to work within your ecosystem.

Empathize—research your users' needs: In the first stage of the design thinking process you go deep into your users' needs to develop an empathetic understanding of the problems you're trying to solve. Empathy is crucial to a human-centered design process because it allows you to set aside your own assumptions about the world and gain real insight into users and their needs.

Define—state your users' needs and problems: During this stage, you accumulate the information gathered during the empathize stage and analyze your observations. As you begin to define problems, you are, in effect, synthesizing your discoveries to identify the problems you will need to design for as you build your ecosystem.

Don't automate what you do—automate to do it better: Automating how you, your team, or your organization are currently doing things can be valuable. But approaching automation in this way might blind you to important opportunities in hyperautomation. Nine times out of 10 it will be more valuable to your company if you create automation that reflects the ideal way of getting things done, rather than how they're currently being done.

Ideate—challenge assumptions and create ideas: Now it's time to bring your defined problems into the ideation stage. This means lots of brainstorming with everyone involved in the project thinking outside the box. There are no wrong answers, as alternative approaches to the problem statements you've created are likely to lead to innovation.

Prototype—start to create solutions: During this phase, the design team produces a variety of inexpensive, scaled-down versions of the product or the features that make up the product in order to investigate different ideas from the ideation phase.

Test—try out your solutions: The viable solutions that come out of the prototype phase can now be tested with users. This is the final stage in the process, but as solutions are tested, it will likely mean a return to the prototype phase to tinker with designs. Future iterations will improve on what works and remedy what doesn't. Iterate until the cows come home—this is an infinite loop.

Iterate! It's probably already clear by now, but iteration is key if not central to this process. If you're truly operating a design strategy that values user-centered principles, omniscience is your enemy. The name of the game will be getting to the point where you have a thing to iterate on as quickly as possible. Once you have a thing to test and observe, iterate, iterate again, and iterate some more.

Design thinking is ideal for tackling the convoluted problems of hyperautomation, where it's difficult to identify the human needs at their core. The more people in your organization who take part in applying these complex problems, the better!

Key Takeaways

- Hyperautomation efforts hinge on the effectiveness of your core enablement team—the people who facilitate all aspects of hyperautomation and, more importantly, get everyone in your organization comfortable creating and improving their own automations.

- The core enablement team is composed of variations of several familiar roles plus the addition of the new strategic liaison (SL) role—the person who binds the work being done by the core enablement team to the fabric of your organization.

- A typical day in the life of an SL involves meeting with different departments throughout your organization, addressing specific concerns, fueling the culture of co-creation, and empowering everyone to take part in the pursuit of hyperautomation.

Visit Invisiblemachines.ai for more information on building a core enablement team for hyperautomation.

CHAPTER 11

Preparing Tools and Architecture

There's a reason people use mountain-climbing metaphors to describe undertakings of this size and scope. Achieving hyperautomation can feel Everest-esque—an outsized challenge shrouded in toil and peril.

Reaching the summit is a coordinated effort that requires a clear vision and strategy. Like a mountain climber, you need to plan ahead to cover all your bases, and you need the right tools. You don't want to find yourself in flip-flops at the base of Everest. Or, to mix metaphors, you don't want to launch into the vast ocean of hyperautomation in a dinghy. When building the ecosystems I'm describing, you need tools that give you total control of iterating and fine-tuning solutions. It's all about feasibility and optionality, which boils down to an open system that puts your organization in charge of its own development cycles.

Tools for hyperautomation efforts—and especially conversational applications—generally fit into one of three categories:

Toolkits: Toolkits are the raw parts that make up conversational experiences. They're wielded by people with deep experience who want to fine-tune or even build their own platforms. As such, toolkits are very time-consuming and require a clear plan. They also tend to be restrictive. Google-owned Dialogflow, for instance, is designed to work with other Google AI tools.

Point solutions: Machines designed for specific scenarios are the most common types of tools in the marketplace. But while they may meet existing needs, they aren't going to outshine the customer experiences offered by your competitors. Such tools are also very easy to outgrow—in fact, you should expect to: since they can't meet the requirements of rapid iteration cycles, they would hamper your capacity to expand. Consider such solutions demos that you should not invest much in as you will likely soon rip it out.

Platforms: If they're built well, platforms occupy the middle ground of complexity. Good platforms are easier to implement than toolkits but are more intensive than point solutions—and they offer night-and-day differences in flexibility. A proper platform for hyperautomating is an open system that allows you to orchestrate and sequence any AI product however you want. These kinds of platforms do about 80% of the work, leaving about 20% for you to customize (though you can take 100% of the credit). The ideal platform serves as a launch point and an accelerator that lets you engender an organization-wide, design-first approach. Beware, however, of point solutions that attempt to expand into platforms. Unless they're offering an open ecosystem that lets you implement any tool you want to use (and not just their suite of solutions), they will restrict your ability to iterate solutions at the rate required for hyperautomating.

At OneReach.ai, during the process of designing a platform for building an ecosystem of intelligent digital workers, my team of mathematicians, linguists, data scientists, UI/UX analysts, and AI scientists huddled together at the foot of our own Mount Everest. At the time, we were essentially using toolkits to build our own platform—and it took a very long time following a very clear vision, executed through constant iteration and adaptation. The hundreds of thousands of hours we spent researching, designing, and developing over 10,000 conversational applications have wrought an open platform for hyperautomating. The more a company is hyperautomating, the more self-driving—and thus, competitive—it becomes.

As I've already suggested, a great fog has been whipped up around the concept of hyperautomation by those who fundamentally understand it differently. Hyperautomation isn't chatbots. It isn't machine learning or even intelligent automation. It isn't NLU, NLP, IVR, or RPA. Hyperautomation isn't the tools—it's the ecosystem and the ways components/elements of the ecosystem are sequenced.

Hyperautomating takes place in an ecosystem that lets you orchestrate freely with these tools (and many others). Getting this kind of ecosystem up and running is a bit of a trust fall because your initial forays will likely fail. From a business standpoint it will probably feel like too big a risk. After all, in a world dominated by GUIs, a simple application that does one or two things well is considered a success. In conversational design, however, a solution that can do only one thing is almost certainly a failure.

Simple chatbots, NLU, IVRs, and RPA have frankly never been good enough to achieve hyperautomation. The key design principle behind successful conversational applications and ecosystems for hyperautomation is to strive for better than human experiences (BtHX). Up until recently, conversational AI was something that companies implemented because the cost savings it afforded outweighed the negative effects of the subpar experience it provided. We've entered an era where a conversational interface will become the primary entry point into your organization (often for both customers and employees). In order to succeed, this kind of interface needs to connect to everything and do a great many things. Really, the only way to approach something so vast and all-encompassing is to fail faster than you've ever failed before.

To temporarily swap out the mountain-climbing metaphor, consider the stand-up comedian. The polished hour of interwoven bits didn't materialize fully formed from the comedian's mind. Comedians routinely take the terrifying first step of dragging fresh ideas up on stage—and then experience their gruesome failures—knowing that this painful process will lead to incremental improvements. Since these improvements are so intimately connected with the real-time reactions they spark, they can only happen through iteration. Over time, the iterative improvements render a rich tapestry of experience. The more accustomed comedians become to this uncomfortable and unpredictable process, the more they can thrive in the discomfort. Hyperautomation is no different.

This idea of failing forward is central to iterative project management schemes such as Agile, but hyperautomation requires even more speed and flexibility. Agile organizations will certainly have a head start, in the very least because design thinking and a willingness to try new ideas are essential to hyperautomation, but the development cycles I'm talking about will move by measures of hours, not days or weeks. The best bet for any organization entering this race is to select tools that are future-proof—tools that give you total control over both the other tools you want to use and how you want to use them.

***

According to Deloitte, larger companies are seeing the end of AI's "early adopter" phase and the beginning of the "early majority" phase. IDC predicts more than $110 billion in spending on AI technologies in 2024. "Companies will adopt AI—not just because they can, but because they must," said Ritu Jyoti, program vice president, Artificial Intelligence at IDC.[1] Companies are becoming more sophisticated in their buying and are looking for powerful, flexible options. Enter CSG2.

Communication Studio G2

The OneReach.ai platform, Communication Studio G2 (CSG2), is a no-code hyperautomation environment for rapidly creating conversational applications. It was designed specifically to facilitate the sequencing of any open AI technologies and to operate over any channel. When you can reach customers through the channel they prefer (or the channel that's nearby), your machine becomes invisible. An omnichannel presence creates incredible power and flexibility. My goal has always been to use that power and flexibility to support conversational experiences between humans and machines or machines and other machines—and we've succeeded. In Gartner's inaugural 2022 Magic Quadrant for Enterprise Conversational AI Platforms, we were named a leader for our Completeness of Vision and Ability to Execute and CSG2 was the highest-scoring platform in Gartner's first Critical Capabilities for Enterprise Conversational AI Platforms report. We also received the top score in four out of five use cases (Customer Service, Human Resources, Voice Bot on Call Center, and Orchestration of Multiple Employee-Facing Bots), and received the second-highest score in the IT Service Desk use case.

Our dedication to openness and flexibility isn't the only reason we're highly acclaimed; my platform excels because it was built around user experience. It's a common mistake with emerging technologies—such as machine learning, process mining, and natural language processing—to put the primary focus on the emerging technologies themselves. I was a pioneer in experience design, as were core members of my team, and we focused on designing rewarding journeys for creating, implementing, and using solutions.

I'm proud to have had luminaries such as Gartner, Fast Company, the Edison Awards, and Deloitte put our conversational AI platform on a pedestal beside global innovators such as SpaceX, Dyson, and IBM as well as key players in AI such as Microsoft, Amazon, and Google. Still, I get a bigger thrill from seeing organizations discover the possibilities CSG2 can unlock and the barriers it can break down.

Through my work, I've become more connected with the different needs of different organizations, along with the different ways those needs can be met. What follows is a practical examination of the kinds of tools and architecture that can be used to bring hyperautomation to life. Because CSG2 was designed specifically to support the sequencing of conversational AI and other technologies for achieving hyperautomation, it will be referenced to guide you up your Mount Everest.

Microservices at the Core

The scale of automation I'm talking about is achieved using microservices. By breaking down a skill into its component services and then breaking those down into their component steps, you get sets of pliable, infinitely customizable microservices. Within an intelligent ecosystem, microservices can be pulled from anywhere in the shared library, modified, sequenced, and deployed—creating new automations as well as new microservices that can be continually iterated on, resequenced, and redeployed.

In terms of defining the shape of an ecosystem, microservices map to flows. These flows of sequenced microservices make up the services and skills that an IDW utilizes. A robust ecosystem has an array of skills that can be sequenced in all sorts of ways. Here's how this works within an automated ecosystem.

***

Sarah is a sales associate for an auto parts provider, and she needs callers to authenticate themselves before placing an order. Her core enablement team (see chapter 10) has been like a sherpa, guiding her organization onward and upward, and she's been trained and empowered to use her platform's code-free tools to create new services and skills.

Sarah wants to train an IDW to perform her current authentication workflow for wholesale buyers calling in. To Sarah, creating automated workflows feels about as technical as creating a mildly complex spreadsheet. It's not an intimidating process because it involves no coding; in fact, there's very little visible technology in her journey. Her challenge is the fact that the solution will come quickly, and fine-tuning the experience of using the solution will take lots and lots of iteration.

She finds an authentication skill in the shared library, but it doesn't operate in precisely the way she needs. (Relying on SMS to authenticate won't work for her wholesale buyers, since many of them are in countries where SMS is less reliable.) So she looks through the flow of the skill, finds the microservices that facilitate the SMS component of the workflow, and replaces them with steps that use WhatsApp instead. Now the newly created automation functions exactly the way she needs it to.

In the next phase, the QA on Sarah's core enablement team can help her test the prototyped automation. She and the XD will also want to refine it together using her journey maps—marking the beginning of this skill's evolution. Once the automation is activated, it becomes a time-saver, and Sarah feels empowered to create more automations (with less assistance). The automation is also added to the organization's shared library so that others can borrow and iterate from it. The skill can also be fine-tuned at will; no one will have to wait for an outside development team to make the necessary updates. (Sarah finds this fact particularly liberating given how often she's been hampered by a vendor's development cycles; plus, she knows how coworkers can be wary of tinkering with a proprietary tool and breaking its functionality.)

Thanks to the work of the core enablement team, Sarah is just one of many employees, working across departments, who are able to build new automations by designing and sequencing microservices in new ways. All combined, the capacity to design and implement strategic automations gives customers and team members rewarding experiences that enhance their output.

Remember, however, that code-free creation is just a tool. In the same way that learning to code alone doesn't make you a programmer, having access to code-free creation doesn't mean much unless you know how to use it. In this example, Sarah's expertise in the processes unique to her role and department allows her to create successful software. Code-free creation is nothing more than a party trick if you don't understand how to leverage it to solve problems in an optimized way. For example, someone can prop up an impressive-looking piece of software quickly and easily, but the depth of that software is entirely dependent on how well it addresses a real need. With tools that are more open, fast, and accessible in the hands of people who understand the tasks you want to automate, your organization can build automations that are ready faster, easier to deploy, reusable, and highly scalable.

This method of software design requires a balance, however. With code-free creation, if the modular pieces are too large, the solutions will be less flexible. If the pieces are too small, they can quickly become too complex for non-developers to succeed with. Achieving and maintaining this balance takes a coordinated effort across departments. This is what I mean when I say that AI is a team sport. It requires interplay among people who understand the processes being automated and those who understand how those automations can be generated within the complex integrated ecosystems I'm prescribing.

IDEA IN BRIEF: Microservices, Your New Best Friend

An ecosystem built for hyperautomating relies on the flexibility and interchangeability of microservices, the building blocks of your skills available to anyone in your organization through the shared library. Here's why you will love them.

Ready faster: Since development cycles are shortened, microservices architecture supports more agile deployment and updates.

(continued)

Highly scalable: As demand for certain services grows, you can sequence and deploy microservices across multiple servers and infrastructures to meet your needs.

Resilient: When constructed properly, independent microservices don't affect one another. This means that if one piece fails, the whole IDW doesn't go down.

Easy to deploy: Because your microservice-based apps are modular and smaller than monolithic apps, the worries that came with traditional deployment are negated. Microservices require more coordination, but the payoffs can be huge.

Fast and accessible: Because the larger app is broken down into smaller pieces, developers can more easily understand, update, and enhance those pieces, resulting in faster development cycles—especially when combined with hyper-agile development methodologies. This also makes it easier to get distributed teams working together.

Reusability: Microservices can be sequenced in different ways with different sets of other microservices to create new skills and services. They can also be tweaked within existing sequences to produce different outcomes.

More open: The use of polyglot APIs gives developers the freedom to choose the best language and technology for the necessary function.

Orchestrating Hyperautomation Requires an Open System

In an ecosystem built for hyperautomation, conversation is the tissue that connects all the individual nodes at play. A state of hyperautomation within an organization is achieved when a collection of advanced technologies are sequenced in perpetually intelligent ways to create automations of business processes that continue getting smarter. In these ecosystems, machines are communicating with other machines, but there are also conversations between humans and machines. Inside truly optimized ecosystems, humans are training their digital counterparts to complete new tasks through conversational interfaces—they're telling them how to contextualize and solve problems.

These innovations, algorithms, and systems that get sewn together start to build what's referred to as general intelligence, or perceived general intelligence, by having access to everybody's tools. This won't happen inside a closed system where the tools have to be supplied exclusively by Google or IBM. For instance, if you're handcuffed to a specific NLP or NLU vendor, your development cycles will be limited by their schedule and capabilities. This is actually a common misstep for organizations looking for vendors: it's easy to think that the processing and contextualization of natural language *is* artificial intelligence. But NLP/NLU is just one piece of technology that makes up an ecosystem for creating artificial intelligence. Perhaps more importantly, in terms of keeping an open system, NLP/NLU is one of many modular technologies that can be orchestrated within an ecosystem. "Modular" means that, when better functionalities—like improved NLP/NLU—emerge, an open system is ready to accept and use them.

In the rush to begin hyperautomating, NLP/NLU and conversational AI are often the first stumbling block for organizations. As they attempt to automate specific aspects of their operations, the result is usually a smattering of chatbots each operating on their own closed system that are unable to become part of an orchestrated effort—and thus create subpar user experiences.

Think of auto manufacturing. In some ways, it would be easier to manage the supply chain if everything came from one supplier or if the manufacturer supplied its own parts, but production would suffer. Ford—a pioneer of assembly-line efficiency—relies on a supply chain with over 1,400 tier 1 suppliers separated by up to 10 tiers between supply and raw materials, providing significant opportunities to identify and reduce costs and protect against economic shifts.[2] This represents a viable philosophy where hyperautomation is concerned as well. Naturally, it comes with a far more complex set of variables, but relying on one tool or vendor stifles nearly every aspect of the process: innovation, design, user experience—it all suffers.

"Most of the high-profile successes of AI so far have been in relatively closed sorts of domains," Dr. Ben Goertzel said in his TEDx-Berkeley talk, "Decentralized AI," pointing to game playing as an example. He describes AI programs playing chess better than any human but reminds us that these applications still "choke a bit when you give them the full chaotic splendor of the everyday world that we live in."

Goertzel has been working in this frontier for years through the OpenCog Foundation, the Artificial General Intelligence Society, and SingularityNET, a decentralized AI platform which lets multiple AI agents cooperate to solve problems in a participatory way without any central controller.

In that same TEDx talk, Goertzel references ideas from Marvin Minsky's book *The Society of Mind*: "It may not be one algorithm written by one programmer or one company that gives the breakthrough to general intelligence. . . . It may be a network of different AIs each doing different things, specializing in certain kinds of problems."[3]

Hyperautomating within an organization is much the same: a whole network of elements working together in an evolutionary fashion. As the architects of the ecosystem are able to iterate rapidly—trying out new configurations—the fittest tools, AIs, and algorithms survive. From a business standpoint, these open systems provide the means to understand, analyze, and manage the relationships between all of the moving parts inside your burgeoning ecosystem, which is the only way to craft a feasible strategy for achieving hyperautomation.

Creating an architecture for hyperautomation is a matter of creating an infrastructure—not so much the individual elements that exist within an infrastructure. It's the roads, electricity, and waterways that you put in place to support houses and buildings and communities. That's the problem a lot of organizations have with these efforts. They're failing to see how vast it is. Simulating human beings and automating tasks are not the same as buying an email marketing tool.

The beauty of an open platform is that you don't have to get it right. It might be frightening in some regards to step outside a neatly bottled or more familiar ecosystem, but the breadth and complexity of AI are also where its problem-solving powers reside. Following practical wisdom applied to emergent technologies—wait until a clear path forward emerges before buying in—won't work because once one organization achieves a state of hyperautomation, their competitors won't be able to catch them. By choosing one flavor or system for all of your conversational AI needs, you're limiting yourself at a time when you need as many tools as you can get. The only way to know what tools to use is to try them all, and with a truly open system, you have the power to do that.

Using a tool such as CSG2, the technology has been abstracted, leaving Sarah in a place where she doesn't have to worry about the architecture or what's behind it. She can just focus on creating the experience. While being recognized by Gartner ahead of giant corporations such as IBM and Amazon remains a huge honor for my organization, it was also validation that an open system like the one I built is the only realistic approach to hyperautomation.

With the benefits of an open system, Sarah essentially removes the need for developers, becoming a programmer herself—one who doesn't need to code. (This, by proxy, makes the software developers on her team into super-programmers.) Sarah is creating and templating new skills that can be vetted for quality assurance and standards by the core enablement team before being submitted to their company's shared library, where they can be resourced by her coworkers for their IDWs.

By conceiving of an automation, sequencing the right microservices to bring it to life, and sharing the skill with her entire organization (all without writing any code), Sarah is able to apply her hands-on knowledge of a workflow to the training of an IDW thoughtfully and efficiently, while also adding to the capability of the ecosystem as a whole.

As you can imagine, this distributed development and deployment of microservices gives your entire organization a massive boost. You can also create multiple applications/skills concurrently, meaning more developers working on the same app, at the same time, resulting in less time spent in development. All of this activity thrives because the open system allows new tools from any vendor to be sequenced at will.

Cover All Your Bases

Creating and managing an ecosystem of intelligent digital workers can be an extremely complex undertaking. I designed our platform to mitigate the challenges that are unique to this approach. By making sure you've got these bases covered, you can focus on enabling non-developers to orchestrate conversational and non-conversational advanced technology quickly and easily. This will help you prepare for the unique challenges that come with microservices architecture.

Building: As you organize flows, it's important to identify dependencies between your services. Be aware that changing one microservice might affect other microservices due to dependencies. You also need to consider the effects that microservices have on your data and how changes to your data to suit one microservice might affect other microservices that rely on the same data.

Testing: Integration and end-to-end testing are very important. Depending on how you've architected your services and flows to support one another, a failure in one part of the architecture could cause something a few hops away to fail.

Versioning: When you update to new versions, keep in mind that you might break things if there's no backward compatibility. You can build in conditional logic to handle this, but that can get unwieldy and nasty fast if not managed properly. You can also stand up multiple live versions using different flows, but that can be more complex to maintain and manage.

Logging: With a distributed system, you need centralized logs to bring everything together. Otherwise, the scale is impossible to manage. A centralized view of the system allows you to pinpoint problems. CSG2 does much of this for you, but you'll have to manage occurrences beyond built-in events, errors, and warnings.

Debugging: When it comes to errors reported through user interaction, it can be difficult to pinpoint the microservice that failed if no error or warning log is reported. Automating simple applications such as chatbots, RPAs, or IVRs is relatively easy, but when you take it to the level where you introduce context, memory, and intelligence, identifying bugs beyond errors or warnings can get very complicated.

Compliance and security: When applying technology this powerful and expansive, organizations will need to make sure their plan focuses close attention on any potential compliance and security issues. The fact that ecosystems built for hyperautomating are open systems that use various independent technologies sequenced together and sharing information can pose unique challenges specific to individual organizations. There's no one-size-fits-all cover for this base.

Infrastructure Topology for Conversational AI

The experts, software development time, and dollars required for building production-ready and secure conversational AI applications puts this out of reach for most companies (see Figure 11.1). Once you've covered all the bases in this chapter, operationalizing can be inclusive, fast, and scalable—without sacrificing flexibility.

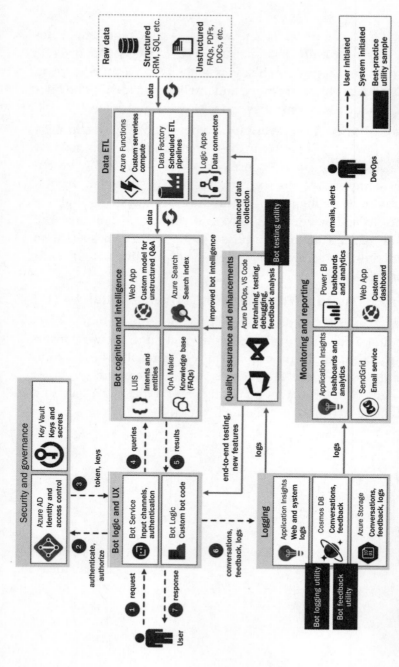

FIGURE 11.1 *Sample ecosystem architecture.* **(https://docs.microsoft.com/en-us/azure/architecture/reference-architectures)**

TOPOLOGY AT A GLANCE

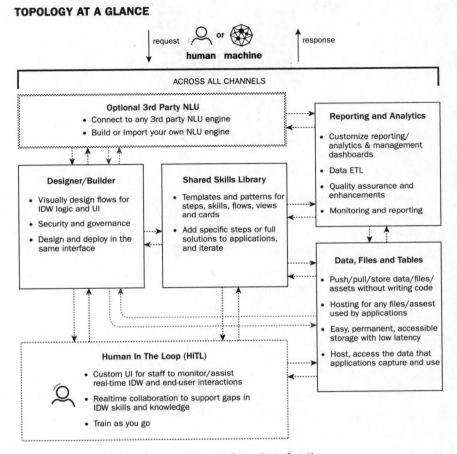

FIGURE 11.2 *Topology at a glance. (OneReach.ai)*

Feasibility Is All About Speed

You need to equip yourself to rapidly generate great conversational experiences—powered by the latest AI—across any channel. Ideas for great experiences are inspired and rarely planned; therefore, the key to great experiences is rapid iteration, not waterfall approaches. When it comes to hyperautomating, speed is the game. In fact, we're covering all these bases to create a foundation for speed. The more you iterate, the better the end experience becomes. The faster you can iterate, the faster your experiences will be better.

Scan to view the current version of this.

Leonard Cohen wrote his song "Hallelujah" over 70 different ways before releasing it. Even then, he still wasn't convinced it was done—*much in the same way that your conversational experiences will never be "done."* Great conversational experiences aren't usually created in a diagram or a spreadsheet and then handed to a developer to be built. They are the result of prototyping, iterating, user testing, scrapping everything, and starting over.

There's a difference between great experiences and sophisticated experiences. In the realm of automation, the latter comes through evolution. You can't sit down and design a sophisticated experience in a fell swoop.

This is why speed matters when it comes to making great experiences. Iterating toward great experiences is hard in any context, let alone in this new and complex world of hyperautomation. You need to be sure your tools make it as easy as possible to prototype, iterate, and test. Whatever platform you use to facilitate hyperautomation needs to be built with speed as the primary factor. I built CSG2 to employ a more agile approach to creating conversational applications; one that allows people with varying technical abilities to work together to easily create great conversational experiences in a matter of days, not months.

Equipping Yourself for Designing and Expanding Skills and IDWs

Imagine you're halfway up Mount Everest and you reach a vertical ice wall. You might be able to scramble up it with some ropes and crampons, but your whole team could ascend it much faster with an ice pick specially designed for the purpose.

I designed our platform with tools specifically tailored for creating an intelligent digital ecosystem where information can be shared easily and intelligently and where improvements can be made by anyone in your organization. You can find other tools that more or less equip you for each of the bases you'll need covered—but to build a code-free ecosystem that embraces co-creation, you need them all, and they need to function together. The considerations outlined below are best handled using tools specialized for maximum efficiency.

When people across your organization automate tasks and create their own skills and microservices, your shared library continues to grow as a resource for other creators and IDWs in the ecosystem. This creates the conditions for your ecosystem to expand and evolve organically. It's not unlike a universe unto itself, with an ever-expanding number of microservices that can be sequenced to meet any problem.

Here are some of the specialized tools you need in order to get to that state.

> **Human-in-the-loop:** Humans need to be able to monitor IDWs as they work, entering into the experience when the machine doesn't know what to do or needs guidance. The IDW can learn from the ongoing process of human-led refinement of automated tasks.
>
> The continued evolution and expansion of an ecosystem relies on the human-in-the-loop process. Humans are a critical part of

FIGURE 11.3   *Three-quarter view of an IDW and it's skills with height indicating increased sophistication.*

the ecosystem, working seamlessly alongside their IDWs, asking one another for help, querying, and establishing recommended responses and actions.

In order to contribute to AI-training and step in where human-touch is needed, people need the ability to moderate IDW-managed conversations in real time.

From these in-experience interventions, IDWs can learn from the live human-to-human interactions—as the member of your organization guides a user to the next step, the IDW gains new contextual data. The knowledge and skills retained by IDWs through in-line training can be leveraged across your organization.

The more time IDWs spend learning from their human counterparts, the faster the ecosystem can evolve. They become more capable and require less human intervention, freeing humans to move on to automating more tasks. Opportunities also emerge for something I call co-botting, where people and IDWs design or modify skills together. This could be as simple as a human realizing they should train an IDW on how to collect payment before a service is rendered.

On the flip side of that example, an IDW looking at analytics data and seeing that a significant number of users are requesting the option to prepay can reach out to a human peer for training on how to complete the transaction.

Shared library: Our old friend the shared library is the central resource of your ecosystem. Everyone draws microservices, skills, and flows from it, and when these elements are customized for new services, that information becomes part of the shared resource. The shared library is crucial for hyperautomating. It supplies your organization with best practices to scale knowledge sharing, accelerate development, and, at the same time, take control of security, compliance, monitoring, best practices, consistency, and scalability.

Actionable documentation: It's crucial to have accurate documentation for your shared library. Documentation enables members of your organization to understand which skills and microservices are available and operational as well as how to use them as they create new solutions.

Quickly build and iterate on primary skills: As you're creating IDWs, you need to be able to quickly build and iterate on primary skills, like being able to operate over any number of specific communication channels (Slack, phone, SMS, Alexa, email, web chat, etc.). Understanding natural language is also a primary skill for an IDW, as is being able to include a human-in-the-loop when necessary.

Views, dashboards, and widgets: It's imperative that you have the ability to generate custom reporting views, dashboards, and widgets that tie into your conversational experiences. These are used to trigger automated tasks and can offer real-time analysis and adaptations driven by your data. Equip your conversational applications to adjust the experiences they offer as they are happening, based on analysis and triggered events in customized reports.

Draw from multiple knowledge bases: If you're attempting to integrate an existing conversational application into your emergent ecosystem, you'll need a tool that can give IDWs access to multiple knowledge bases—a knowledge garden, if you will. For example, imagine an IDW that is equipped to utilize a knowledge base your HR team built, as well as a knowledge base run through IBM Watson and one that you're licensing from your HR applicant tracking software. At some point, you might also need to bring a third-party application into the mix so, once again, you need a tool with the flexibility to do so.

CSG2 was designed with this capability in mind, making it easy to not only integrate third-party applications but to also build your own internal knowledge bases.

Easy access to stored data: It's important to have easy, permanent, accessible storage for the data your conversational applications capture and use with low latency. You want tools that are designed and optimized to make hosting and accessing data easier on the back end, as users interact with your IDWs. By connecting your automated experiences to APIs or your own files, sheets, and data, you can support their flows. You'll need to be able to push, pull, and store data without writing a line of code.

End-to-end control over voice: The integrity of your audio is crucial when working with conversational AI. Rewarding experiences with NLP, NLU, and IVR require reliable audio quality from the customer's connection point through to your agents. When selecting voice-enabled technology, make sure you choose a platform that gives you end-to-end control of every interaction. That's the only way to effectively troubleshoot problems as they arise and create new solutions effectively. With end-to-end control, you can prototype, test, view traffic, manage channels and APIs, and handle reporting all in one place. In a similar vein, it's also important to be wary of voice gateways. Using a Zoom meeting as an example, if everyone present is using the Zoom app to connect, then Zoom can control the quality of the connections. Anyone who calls into the meeting on a remote telephone line, is accessing through a voice gateway, and the quality of that connection is out of Zoom's hands.

Whenever possible, have users call in using a controlled line. Imagine how difficult it would be to figure out why calls are dropping off for your end users if your only recourse is to trace lines along a spider's web of technologies and suppliers. In this scenario, you'll likely end up caught in the crossfire as vendors blame one another for the issue. However, if you have end-to-end control over voice inputs, you can use analytics and reporting to chart the traffic flow and see exactly where calls are falling off.

Own your road map: If halfway up your Everest, you realize there's a crucial tool you'll need to get to the next checkpoint, it's far better to have the ability to forge the tool right then and there. Radioing back to basecamp and asking someone to send it up to you means valuable time squandered. CSG2 allows you to build tools as you need them, rather than relying on a platform's development team and losing the time it takes for them to generate a solution.

Use rules-based AI and neural networking together: In the realm of AI, there are often two proposed pathways or models: rules-based or neural networking. There is complexity and ongoing discourse surrounding each approach. Suffice to say that with the right tact and tools, you can combine elements of each, allowing your experience designers to create solutions far faster by reducing the need for massive amounts of training data.

Loading historical data into a machine learning model can create a generalized version of the conversations you've had but doesn't necessarily create good experiences. With the learning capabilities of neural networks and the power of rule-based AI,

XDs can adapt to new settings and problems with far less data. Add human-in-the-loop systems to the mix, and you can cut up-front training data needs to almost zero.

No Code Means Fewer Barriers

Fifty years ago, if you worked on a computer, you almost certainly worked in something called "the computer department." These days, the notion of a computer department is so antiquated that it's foreign. Nearly everyone works on a computer. Now apply that same dynamic to software development. Currently, most companies use third-party software solutions, consulting vendors, or have an internal software development department that builds/codes the software they need. Now imagine a world where anyone can build software solutions (in much the same way everyone can now use a computer).

You won't have to wait 50 years for this world to materialize; this seismic shift is upon us. We're well on our way to the "development department" being a thing of the past—doing away with the time and energy that companies have had to pour into development cycles. Enabling your company to program the automation of business processes, tasks, and communications without writing code eliminates the need for a traditional development cycle and is a key factor that accelerates growth in your ecosystem.

Reaching this point requires defiance. Two particular paradigms need to be shattered within your organization. The first of these is the triple constraint or iron triangle: fast, cheap, or good, you can pick only two. (See Figure 11.4.) The second is the idea that you have to choose between flexibility and usability: if a platform is flexible, it will be difficult to wrangle; if it's easy to use, it will also be rigid. (See Figure 11.5.) Using an open platform, we've smashed these constraint paradigms to smithereens. None of these compromises exist with no-code today, so there's no need to live under their thumbs. My teams have seen more than 10,000 AI applications created by customers, and 80% of the humans using our platform don't know how to write code. When anyone in your organization can take part in the evolution of your ecosystem, you can quickly create solutions that are inexpensive and effective, with no need to choose between usability and flexibility. This is the fast-track toward succeeding in hyperautomation.

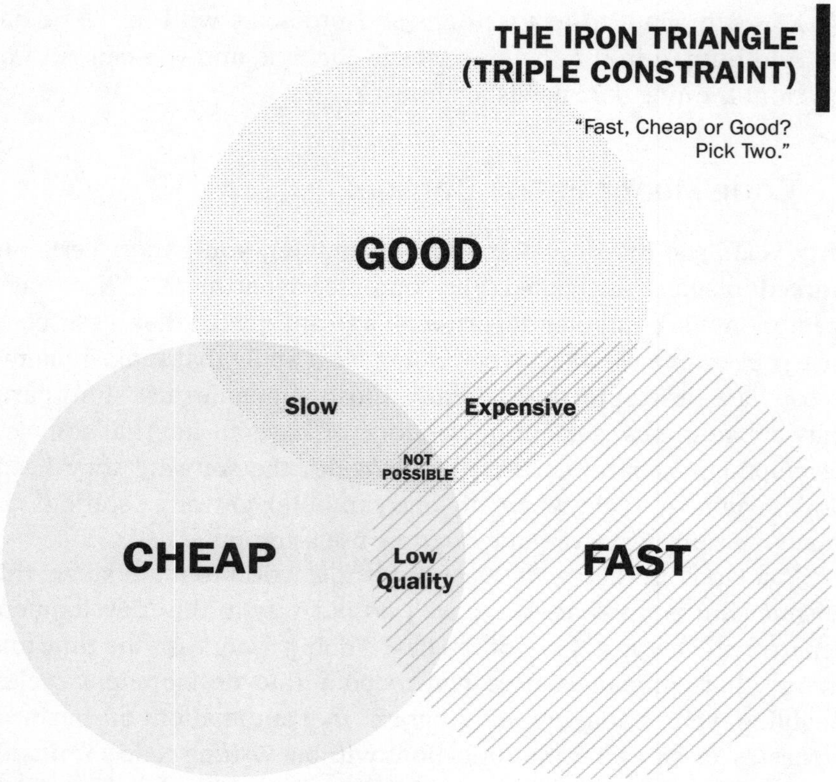

**THE IRON TRIANGLE
(TRIPLE CONSTRAINT)**

"Fast, Cheap or Good?
Pick Two."

GOOD

Slow   Expensive

**NOT
POSSIBLE**

CHEAP   Low
Quality   **FAST**

FIGURE 11.4   *The iron triangle, or triple constraint.*

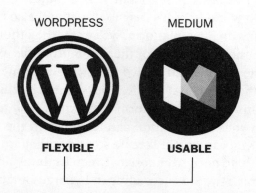

**THE FLEXIBILITY-
USABILITY TRADE-OFF**

"Pick one."

WORDPRESS   MEDIUM

FLEXIBLE   **USABLE**

FIGURE 11.5   *The flexibility-usability trade-off.*

Scan for more on the trade-offs and common constraint paradigms.

Currently, the most efficient way to accelerate the force-multiplying effects of hyperautomation is for your company to equip themselves for rapid code-free programming. As I've outlined, when the technology itself recedes into the background, members of your organization can contribute directly to the automation of tasks they know best; just remember, code-free creation is only a tool, and you need requisite experience to use it. The people closest to your organization's problems will be best equipped to solve them, shifting solutioning closer to those who feel the pain of the problem and are intimate with what the solution should be. Supporting the people who can articulate the process being automated, you need developers who can articulate the granular pieces of the resulting automations. Code-free doesn't mean that the code doesn't exist. In the same way that a conversational interface obscures the messiness behind the scenes for end users, it also obscures the inner workings for those building software.

For another contextual example, think of the way that web design has changed over the past couple of decades. Initially, you needed a fairly in-depth understanding of coding languages to create even a static website. As websites became more interactive and functional, the knowledge required to build them became more complex. Eventually, tools emerged that empowered people without web development skills to build their own sites by customizing existing templates.

Now we're at the point where someone with limited computing skills can build a single-use, multi-page website (one that coordinates information for an upcoming wedding, for example) in a single afternoon. Hyperautomating opens the door to creating single-use software, something I found myself doing recently as my family prepared for a move. We were leaving behind a house in Denver, Colorado, and all of our family's possessions needed to be indexed and boxed, as some things would be waiting for us in Mexico, where we planned to vacation before rendezvousing with the rest of our stuff in Berkeley, California.

Using the platform I designed, I was able to quicky create an IDW that I shared with my wife. The system was rather simple. Either one of us could tell this IDW that we were going to start packing a new box. The IDW would assign that box a number and ask where it was going (Mexico? California? my brother's garage in Colorado?). As we filled the boxes, we could send the IDW photos and/or descriptions of the things going inside. Months later, when I was trying to find my motorcycle helmet, I asked the IDW where it was. The IDW, in turn, was able to tell me which box number it was in and at which location.

I didn't create this piece of single-use software because it was cool or because it allowed me to flex the capabilities of my platform. I did it because it was easy to do and it was going to save me a ton of time. This encapsulates the promise of code-free creation. Devise an automation that will make your life easier, design it on the fly, and then set it aside when you're done with it.

No-code conversational AI platforms let people automate workflows they understand without needing any requisite knowledge—just the ability to converse with a platform through natural language and use simple, visual, drag-and-drop programming. This is precisely why I designed CSG2: to empower users with code-free programming features. Co-creation relies on everyone taking part, and no-code tools let anyone contribute to great software design with rapid results. Always remember: speed is central to staying competitive in this race.

***

This is all a new way to create and manage software. Setting up conversational AI as an interface for no-code creation does something bigger than allowing anyone in an organization to design IDWs. What's really happening when people employ these tools and processes is software creation. In this new paradigm, software isn't created through developers, software solutions are designed (and often implemented) by people who best understand the problems being solved. This scenario finds developers in crucial roles that include advising the organization of high-level technical aspects of their ecosystem as well as making adjustments to skills on a granular level. Here, developers are tasked with creating and extending the tools that the people in their organization use to create and refine software. This represents a radically optimized approach to software creation that, once normalized, will fundamentally change the relationship between business and technology.

Key Takeaways

- Building ecosystems for hyperautomating requires tools that give you total control of iterating and fine-tuning solutions—it's all about feasibility and optionality.
- Hyperautomating requires an open system that lets you use the best tools available and puts your organization in charge of its own development cycles.
- This level of automation is done by breaking skills down into their component services and then breaking those down into their component steps, giving you pliable, infinitely customizable microservices.
- Covering your bases lets you focus on enabling non-developers to orchestrate conversational and non-conversational advanced technology quickly and easily.
- The most efficient way to accelerate the force-multiplying effects of hyperautomation is to equip your organization for rapid, code-free programming.

Visit Invisiblemachines.ai for up-to-date information on the tools being used in hyperautomation.

CHAPTER 12

Vetting Your Vendors

When approaching any vendor in this space, you should be armed with a litany of items to crosscheck: voice and NLU capabilities, channel flexibility, compatibility issues, development cycles—the list spirals on.

Despite the complexity, there's one thing you should find out before asking anything else:

How much of a vendor's own business is run by the same kinds of machines they are selling you? Whether they're a platform vendor or a services vendor, it should be easy for them to show you how they've put their solution to use for themselves.

If they've truly found a way to make hyperautomation sing, people across their entire organization will be creating, using, and iterating on the technology regularly.

The Cobbler's Children Have New Shoes: The Feasibility Vendor Litmus Test

A successful ecosystem of IDWs is such a game changer in terms of efficiency and productivity that if a vendor has figured out how to make complexity feasible in conversational AI, they will definitely be using their own products internally (or if they're a services vendor, they will have a rapidly growing number of valuable examples that everyone internally knows and that they're regularly improving upon). Initiate your assessment by asking vendors these kinds of questions:

- Have you successfully automated internal processes?
- Are your internal machines integral to your own operations? (*Or are they just window dressing?*)
- Are employees within your organization clamoring for more machines because they see automation working?
- What skills and use cases have you tackled? Can you show us?

If a vendor falls back on the old "cobbler's kids go without shoes" adage, be wary. There was a time when my own company used that excuse: that we were too busy creating solutions to put them to use for ourselves. Then I realized what bullshit that excuse is: if I can't get my own employees to use my platform, how can I ever expect a customer to get their employees to use it? With that in mind, my team and I headed back to work to dig deeper and crack the code. We took aim at our most complex internal processes and operations, undertaking the automation of our trickiest bits. That journey is now one I'm eager to share with customers and partners. Not only does it demystify some of the key elements of hyperautomation, it also shows that we know how to put our platform to work. Any vendor worth pursuing should be able to share a similar journey.

If you've already vetted and are working with a vendor, ask yourself this: How quick are my iteration cycles? If it takes more than a week to add a new skill or iterate, you probably need to begin looking elsewhere. Having the right tools in place is paramount to building a functional ecosystem for your IDWs.

There are many platforms and tools out there that can help cover some of the various bases I've outlined and can help facilitate fruitful builds. To the best of my knowledge, CSG2 is currently the only platform that addresses all of the needs I've identified for creating an intelligent ecosystem of digital workers, but that doesn't mean there aren't other ways to go about building one. Here are some helpful guidelines to help you find the right vendor or platform or combination of both.

Keep Asking Vendors Questions

Once a vendor has shown you how they use their tool internally, you can make your search for the right tools a whole lot shorter by asking the right questions up front. You'll most certainly regret spending hours or days exploring a platform only to find out later that it won't meet critical basic requirements for a scalable strategy. Asking the following types of questions can help narrow your search more efficiently.

What types of voice and NLU capabilities do you have?

- Market leadership on NLU is constantly in flux. Can you show that you've future-proofed your NLU?
- Can you utilize multiple STT, TTS, and NLU engines?
- Are you tied to individual NLU platforms and AI engines or is there portability between applications to account for new providers entering the marketplace?

What communication channels can you create conversational experiences on?

- Can you use multiple channels—phone, SMS, MMS, and email—during the same continuous conversation interchangeably while maintaining context?
- Are you tied to specific communication channel providers for channels such as phone, SMS, and WhatsApp, or will your solutions be portable to other similar providers?

What limitations are there surrounding development and deployment?

- What kind of analytics are available to facilitate fast and meaningful iterations?
- How quickly can experiences be created and deployed?
- What skill levels are required to design, develop, deploy, and iterate on solutions and experiences?
- Will you be able to equip non-developers and developers alike to create conversational AI applications and task automation, or will it require developers to build your solutions?

- Will you have access to libraries and templates, or will those need to be built from scratch?
- If the tools and templates you have access to are no-code, how flexible are they?

How hard is it to train new users on the platform?

- What capabilities and controls are accessible to end users? Which aspects are behind the wall?
- What level of investment (in terms of experts, departments, technologies, and timelines) will be needed across all aspects of design and deployment (including development, reporting, security, and scaling)?

Bake-Offs: The New RFP

As a valuation tool, the request for proposal, or RFP, is being jettisoned across industries in favor of bake-offs because the latter approach offers a more hands-on, efficient approach to finding solutions that will meet organizational needs. This is especially true if your goal is hyperautomating. The fastest way to find out if and how a solution can be applied to the problems you want to solve is to see it in action, solving those problems. Comparing the same proof of concept baked on multiple platforms is a great way to find the one that fits.

That's not to say that you shouldn't be thorough. There's a reason that RFPs often stretch past the 100-page mark, and hyperautomation is no less complex than other technological endeavors. (On the contrary—it's uniformly more complex.)

Ultimately, you're in the midst of a process that requires flexibility and speed. For many organizations that haven't yet fully adopted faster, more iterative models for operating, adding a bake-off to the vendor selection or procurement is incredibly valuable, but they're not able to fully replace RFPs with them.

Sending out requests for proposals, waiting for proposals, comparing proposals, and then pursuing the best ones is a long process; add to that an already lengthy gathering and implementation process. A two- or three-day proof of concept bake-off can often accelerate these processes—but for many organizations it is an additive to the RFP process, not a replacement.

Either way, any platform worth its salt will be capable of propping up a sample experience surrounding your needs (especially if they are putting their product to work internally). If they can't do that, chances are their platform isn't going to lend itself well to hyperautomation. I designed CSG2 to be easy enough to use that prototyping and participating in bake-offs is actually quite fun and illuminating.

Remember, hyperautomation hinges on design input from people with varying technical abilities working across your organization. If a solution can't be activated quickly and easily and without heavy technology lifting, it likely won't work well or won't be fast (or both).

Whatever You Do, Don't Overlook UX

The biggest contributor to the abandonment of hyperautomation efforts will be poor user experience—both in the customer-facing solutions and internally. With something as all-encompassing and far-reaching as hyperautomation, usability is the number-one factor affecting the adoption of your strategy, process, and tools. You're better off not attempting hyperautomation at all than going after it with the wrong tools because if people don't adopt your solution, it won't work for hyperautomation.

There are a handful of platforms in this space that openly boast about hiring leading UX consultancies and senior UX staff in order to improve the usability of their platforms. While this has a veneer of respectability, the truth is that if a vendor has built a platform that they need help making usable, they didn't put usability at the core of the efforts to begin with. What they've built will probably suffer from struggling adoption rates, no matter how much talent and money get thrown at it. It's almost universally true that the companies with the best user experience (Apple, Tesla, Lemonade, etc.) forged their operations around experience-design thinking and strategy. Plenty of other companies have passably limped along by slapping together an outer shell of usability that hides a siloed, dysfunctional interior. With hyperautomation, that approach won't even get you off the starting blocks. Successful hyperautomation requires an attention to design that drives to the center of an organization, and platforms for orchestrating hyperautomation need to have usability built in at a foundational level.

My leadership team is made up of experience design pioneers who helped propel and define the discipline back in the early 2000s—creating innovative technologies for companies such as Adobe, Boeing, and FedEx. These are people I've worked with for decades and, combined, we have more than a hundred years of experience in UX. I love a good challenge and, many years ago, ran headlong toward one of the worst experiences people routinely have with technology: interactions with IVRs. Nobody likes dealing with them, and this has long been an underserved area (with no significant innovations since the 1970s)—perhaps because no one had a vision of how to take it on. What began as a research project to determine what was broken and how it could all be fixed and refactored evolved into my own platform for hyperautomation (CSG2). I agree with IBM's proposed fundamental design factors for AI, which states, "Our solutions must primarily address user needs instead of being force-fit to accommodate technical capabilities or requirements."[1]

However, their application is problematic because, currently, IBM's solutions are closed systems where user needs can only be addressed by the technological capabilities or requirements imposed by their own line of solutions. There are very real scenarios where a closed system like IBM's might meet some of your needs, but solutions to other core problems exist outside of that system. At the very least your road map will be defined by theirs. These are the kinds of restrictions that guarantee failure. Gartner predicts that 90% of organizations will abandon their early attempts at hyperautomation due largely to the fact that the speed of artificial intelligence computation doubles every three months, according to Stanford University's 2019 AI Index report. This outpaces Moore's Law, which dictates that processor speeds double every 18–24 months.[2]

This is the nature of the types of disruptive technologies that contribute to successful hyperautomation: they are growing in strength and potential at a highly accelerated rate. A system with the user's needs as a primary concern needs to be open to outside technology because the best solutions for optimizing experiences within an ecosystem built for intelligent hyperautomation could come from anywhere. Right now there's probably a company you've never heard of somewhere in the world designing a tool that you will need to give your users the best automated experience. With an open system, you can incorporate that tool the moment the need arises and begin iterating on how to use it most efficiently. With a closed system, as problems emerge that can't be solved with the internal tool set, you're forced to wait for your vendor to build a solution—a purgatory that can quickly derail key business initiatives. In this sense a closed system has a very low standard for usability. In the broken chatbot landscape, sales and marketing use their budget to start conversations with customers, and call centers are hurling money at bad automated solutions in an effort to avoid conversations with customers. I designed an open platform driven by experience design thinking so that it would be easy to create scenarios where every conversation becomes an opportunity rather than a pain point. I'm not trying to say that you need my platform to succeed with hyper-automation, but you do need one that's open and that was conceived and created with usability in mind. Don't be misled by vendors that claim to be UX centric when all they've really done is addressed usability as an afterthought.

Key Takeaways

- Asking vendors the right questions early on can avoid time wasted exploring solutions that are inadequate for hyperautomation.
- The fastest way to find out if and how a solution can be applied to the problems you want to solve is to see it in action. Comparing the same proof of concept baked on multiple platforms is a great way to find the one that fits.
- If a vendor's solution is great for building these kinds of automations, they'll be using it internally and should be able to quickly point to successful implementations.
- The experience of building on a platform shouldn't be an afterthought. If you can't get your team using a solution, then it's not a solution.

Visit Invisiblemachines.ai for more guidance on selecting the proper vendors for your journey toward hyperautomation.

CHAPTER 13

Articulating Your Strategy to Others

Building a coordinated ecosystem of intelligent digital workers is a complex and sophisticated undertaking that requires a solid strategy. While the implementation of these technologies toward hyperautomation is likely a newer concept to stakeholders, many of the design principles, approaches to problem-solving, and processes are familiar. The biggest challenge you're likely to face is getting the decision makers to accept the fact that this requires involvement from—and potentially the restructuring of—every department inside your organization.

There's also the $1,000 light switch paradox at the center of it all. Putting it in familiar terms, to the outside world, a quest to outfit your house with a voice-controlled light switch might seem ludicrous. Say you need to spend about $500 for a voice-activated smart speaker, $200 for light bulbs you can connect to wirelessly, and $300 for a smartphone to turn them on and off. Why drop a grand to automate a functionality that already works well and requires little effort? What outsiders aren't seeing is that you're laying the foundation for a house full of voice-activated automations.

That's how this journey works. You must be willing to look a little foolish at first. You'll need to make a significant investment and then resign yourself to the fact that the road to hyperautomation involves a lot of baby steps and falling on your face. You need to start small, but small is underwhelming. So far, too many organizations look for a use case that isn't underwhelming and set themselves up for failure—jumping into complex use cases and slapping together machines that are bound to suffer low adoption rates and end up being scrapped.

Your initial successes with automation probably won't seem groundbreaking, but they are foundational pieces that can be improved and built upon for years. Over time, as more and more companies jump on board—and more and more people experience great examples of it being applied—it will become easier to implement and become the obvious choice, with competitors and employees increasingly expecting it. If by the time you read this book those examples are already around you, I'm sorry to say that you're probably far behind, and it will be very difficult to catch up. So start. It's much better to look foolish now than to feel foolish in a few short years, when the moment to seize a golden opportunity has passed.

Start small and start internally. The problems hyperautomation allows an organization to tackle might be the surest ticket in. The benefits people inside and outside of your organization can experience following the implementing of a sound strategy will vary according to their role, but if you can identify specific, feasible use cases, the picture will become clearer. Consider who you're trying to get buy-in and participation from and how advanced automation will solve specific problems that will benefit them. On a larger scale, identify how the strategy you aim to work through will benefit stakeholders. You'll really need them to believe in the idea of AI adoption because while the rewards are vast, the ask is usually quite substantial. Here are four things you can do to create a solid foundation for your argument.

Start working internally: If you're able to, start internally by automating tasks, not jobs. With most organizations, starting internally is the fastest way to accelerate your path to AI adoption. By focusing on employees—on helping them accomplish more and experience more satisfaction with their jobs—you are focusing on your customers.

The simpler you make your starting point, the sooner you can test and iterate. The sooner you test and iterate, the sooner you can roll out an internal solution. By rolling out an internal success, you're demonstrating the process by which AI will get trained and are closer to beginning testing for customer-facing conversational applications.

At this stage, you won't have an ecosystem within which to truly evolve your automations, but you'll have demonstrated how automations are created, making it easier for others to visualize how a key piece of hyperautomation works. You'll also be able to draw connections between your automations and future automations and how an ecosystem enables their continual improvement.

Lead by example: By creating automations internally, you're demonstrating solutions that will improve the way work gets done inside your organization. Leading by example can help getting the people around you invested in (and excited about) the journey you want to take. You'll want as much internal support as you can muster while working toward getting buy-in. Having a deeper understanding of your strategy and a clear point of view for how hyperautomating will accelerate your organization makes it easier to evangelize and persuade people that hyperautomation is the answer.

An empathetic and engaging approach right from the start can provoke the insights and participation needed for shaping the shared vision of what the right solution might look like. This naturally lends itself to people buying into the experiences you intend to create while building collective familiarity and firsthand experience with the processes for creating them.

If you've started simply enough, the biggest up-front ask will be for people's time and participation. You'll need minimal budget for getting access to the tools and training needed to start building a demonstration. If you aren't able to hire or establish a core co-creation enablement team before getting buy-in, step through the process as best you can with people who can serve as informal proxies for the roles that will eventually emerge.

Having empathy for your stakeholders is also important. Avoid preaching about your recommendations and budding expertise. Instead, bring them along for the journey. If you've been creating automations internally, let your co-creators—the people you designed automations with and for—join the conversation. As you move through discovery, demonstration, proof of concept, and pilot, you should be using the co-creation process as guiding rails toward getting buy-in. Co-creation drives the whole process of hyperautomation, so make sure it's part of your bedrock.

Fight the urge to "plan flute": Maybe you've seen the pan flute flowchart out there on the Internet. (See Figure 13.1.) The idea is that, whether your answer to the question "Do I need a pan flute?"

is yes or no, the outcome should always be "no pan flute."[1] "Plan fluting" is a related notion that popped up internally at One-Reach.ai. The idea is that with hyperautomation, the answer to the question of "Do I need to start building?" should always flow to "You should be building"—even if your reply is "I need to spend

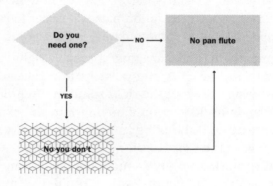

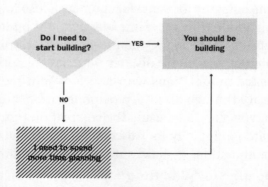

FIGURE 13.1 *Pan flute diagram and "Plan" flute diagram. (OneReach.ai)*

more time planning." This isn't to say that you don't want to go into this with no plan, it means that once you've established your strategy and point of view, what should follow is a ton of trial and error. This might not be welcome news to stakeholders, but 9 times out of 10, it's better to be building (and testing, iterating, and rebuilding) than to be planning. Establish a track record of going with the "You should be building" flow as you create early automations, and you'll be able to help stakeholders avoid playing the plan flute as well.

Let the bot sauce flow: Success with hyperautomation—and conversational design in particular—comes about in an ecosystem that's built for speed and flexibility. Especially when attempting to work at scale, the only feasible way to design conversational experiences that are meaningful to users is to prop solutions up quickly and iterate on them at a rapid pace. At OneReach.ai, we often refer to this process as applying bot sauce. When you're building new solutions using no-code/low code creation tools and devising improved versions as you watch them fail in real time, you're laying on the bot sauce. You can also think of bot sauce as the conversational interface that you're slathering overtop of the pieces of software that make up the underlying experience. A heaping serving of bot sauce is what turns ordinary bots into IDWs. It's literally the one thing in your spice cabinet that goes on anything! These bot sauce metaphors have been helpful in getting our partners and customers familiar with (and excited about) this new paradigm of hyperagile software creation. In fact, it's been so useful that we partnered with a purveyor of hot sauces to make our own Bot Sauce. We're always getting requests for fresh bottles of the stuff (it's quite delicious). We hope this means people are putting Bot Sauce on everything—maybe even while they're dousing it on their designs as well.

The Path to Persuasion

The first real step toward implementing your ecosystem strategy is fostering the understanding that your organization desperately needs one in order to compete in this disruptive—and trending heavily hyperdisruptive—era. You're familiar with what the evolution of an ecosystem looks like and why it matters to your bottom line. The first real marker of progress is when you've developed a vision and plan that will persuade the right people to take the first step with you. Your first real win will be persuading stakeholders to equip you for putting together a demonstration of what it might be like if your company had an IDW to help with a specific need.

Here are some milestones you'll likely need to reach while making the case:

- Claim;
- Grounds;
- Warrant;
- Backing;
- Qualifier;
- Rebuttal;
- Ask.

Thinking through these and doing some homework to know what your version of each might be can provide a helpful launchpad for making the case.

Claim: You're essentially asking stakeholders to accept that your organization should spend a certain amount of money on a preliminary initiative to train, discover, and demonstrate what it might be like if your company had an IDW helping with a specific problem. They should also understand that this is an approach that fosters co-creation of an intelligent ecosystem of coordinated solutions.

Grounds: The data and facts that back up your claim should include concrete examples. For instance, employees spend approximately 1,000 hours per year searching, communicating, and going through processes and formalities in order to get PTO approved, not including their actual PTO time. This equates to about $1,200,000 in staff time per year. The average employee reaches out to support about five times a year in order to get information about forms or processes that they couldn't find in documents or on internal sites. Each of these calls average about 30 minutes. This costs an average of $1,000,000 per year in support center costs and employee time spent getting support.

Warrant: This data is relevant to the claim that addressing these grounds could save the organization more than $300,000 if the initiative produces a 25% decrease in staff time spent searching for information and on calls with support. Approximately $1,000,000 in cost center expenditures.

Backing: This warrant is based on an analysis of employees' attitudes and behaviors in looking for information, which was obtained by cross-referencing an employee survey against site analytics. We discovered that 85% of employees indicated that they experienced frustration during their last attempt at using the company intranet to figure out how to request and get PTO. Of those who reported frustration, 75% contacted support or HR. Analytics show that the average employee looking for PTO-related information in the company intranet clicked an average of 13 pages before ending their journey.

Qualifier: To further qualify the notion that the data backs the warrant and claim, reference relevant expert opinions and/or relevant case studies. Example: cite a thought leader who notes that time spent by employees requesting PTO and related support requests is one of the most overlooked opportunities for reducing cost.

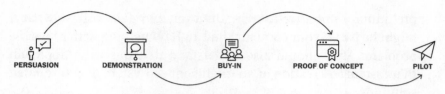

FIGURE 13.2   *Persuasion, demonstration, buy-in, proof of concept, pilot.*

Scan for the current version and more on this topic.

Rebuttal: Your budget is likely to be challenged or questioned. Try explaining the risks associated with not moving forward, recapping the claim and grounds. Example; The proposed initial project will cost about $500,000 to complete and is 90% likely to cut cost by 75% (or $3.71 million). State the minimal risk in taking on one-time costs in order to pursue promising potential solutions to reduce ongoing costs and employee dissatisfaction that, in comparison, are much larger costs and ongoing.

Ask: Here is where you want to get specific about what you'll need for your proposed initiative. Example; You're asking for a $500,000 staff resource commitment: 100 hours of training time, 300 hours of co-creation process time, and 50 hours of stakeholder time. If you've successfully persuaded stakeholders, it's time to get your demonstration ready. If done well, this can propel you across the finish line (and to the starting line, as it were).

Demonstration: The objective of a demonstration is to get participants excited and connected with the possibilities, in order to get buy-in for a proof of concept. Craft a happy-path demonstration, wherein participants don't try the experience. Instead, you show them the experience, by walking them through it. Show them what's possible, not by demonstrating specific solutions or experiences you aim to implement but by reinforcing the possibilities and flexibility automation will afford.

Buy-in: Your demonstration should aim to convert those you've already persuaded. Their buy-in will let you move through a proof of concept.

Proof of concept: A successful proof of concept convinces stakeholders to authorize a pilot phase. Create a proof of concept for guided play—where stakeholders really do try out the specific experience that you would like their buy-in for. The concept of guided play is important and often means providing participants with a journey map they can follow in order to stay on the path of the specific experiences you'd like them to buy into.

Pilot: Once you've earned buy-in for a pilot, you should already be in position to put your strategic process into practice. Ideally, you know what your process looks like and are primed to create an intelligent, coordinated ecosystem of intelligent digital workers that share skills, powered by co-creation across your organization.

Key Takeaways

- Building an ecosystem of intelligent digital workers is complex and demands a clear strategy, and your biggest challenge will likely be getting decision makers to accept that it requires significant involvement from every department inside your organization.
- The best way to lay the groundwork for your plans for hyper-automation is to start leading by example and create automations internally, co-creating with other members of your organization and setting the tone for an always-building, always-improving culture.
- There are key markers on the pathway to persuasion—pay attention to how you move past them and advance toward the next.

Visit Invisiblemachines.ai for more information on hyper-automation.

PART III

Building an Ecosystem of Intelligent Digital Workers

Again, building an ecosystem of intelligent digital workers is all about strategy. To be clear, when I use the word "strategy" I'm not referring to the mission or ultimate goal. This isn't a race to build a static piece of technology; the race is to equip your team and company for faster adoption and iteration of new technologies, skills, and functions.

I believe that the best way to give you a full understanding of an intelligent ecosystem of digital workers is by first unlocking the process behind building one. When I talk about hyperautomation, I'm talking about sequencing tasks and technologies in ways that reveal unseen potential and multiply outcomes. When you step back to consider the vast multitude of technologies and tasks that make up an organization and imagine the countless ways they might be sequenced together, the complexity of the situation can quickly overwhelm. With the right strategy and process, however, you can get everyone in your organization iterating on these sequences, creating a fertile ecosystem for hyperautomation.

CHAPTER 14

The Process of Hyperautomating

If you've worked in neighborhoods adjacent to software design, then likely Agile is no stranger to you. Though it's often misrepresented as a process, Agile is actually a cultural mindset within an organization—one that embraces discovery through shared experimentation, failure, and iteration. Hyperautomation represents the evolution of software design; accordingly, the process that brings it to life requires a mindset and culture that are even more agile than Agile.

Even certified scrum masters might be surprised by how quickly we sprint while creating and iterating in pursuit of hyperautomation. Whereas, if Agile is something you've never applied, the hyperautomation process will feel like massive upheaval. Either way, the key is to internalize the true nature of hyperautomation. This isn't a software design scenario with weekly or monthly product milestones; this process allows you to experiment on active skills, continuously improving them while also activating new skills, multiple times, every day. Part of what makes this possible is an analytics-and-reporting paradigm that provides user data and feedback in real time. Beyond seeing how people are interacting with your conversational interface as those interactions unfurl, you'll also be able to see what kinds of functionalities they're asking for that don't currently exist. These are the kinds of insights that would take weeks (or even longer) to ferret out of a GUI—and they'll be at your disposal immediately. This sets the stage for rapid iteration cycles.

As with traditional Agile scrums, teamwork is the secret sauce when working with AI. As the team at OneReach.ai likes to refer to it, AI is a team sport. Hyperautomation requires collaboration across every department within an organization, and ideas for improving skills *should* come from every department. Everyone will be equipped with basic knowledge about how their organization's ecosystem works, and everyone can co-create alongside the core enablement team we met in Part II. The visceral truth is that this process requires organizations to live/breathe/excrete Agile from every pore. To take the scrum metaphor back into the realm of rugby, all heads need be touching and arms interlocked for a never-ending scrum toward uprights that keep moving away—for this is a shared journey with no defined destination. If your team can't be more agile than Agile, or if AI isn't a team sport in your organization, it's akin to walking on to a rugby pitch as a one-person team and believing you have even a remote chance of winning the match.

If you were to heave the task of building a scalable conversational UI for your ecosystem onto a handful of designers, architects, and developers, no matter how experienced they were, it could take years to unearth the best ways to automate your organization. A proper strategy for hyperautomation includes everyone in your workforce leveraging the individual areas of expertise each employee has to forge optimal sequences and flows.

Starting small and internally is often the easiest way to begin the process. By working directly with employees to automate specific tasks, you begin setting up the structure for future automation. You can continuously improve on automations with the people who understand the specific tasks—and, because these initial applications won't be customer-facing, you can build, test, iterate, test, iterate, test, and deploy as frequently as needed. The better your organization becomes at rolling out successful skills and internal automations, the faster your skills, IDWs, and ecosystem will evolve.

As you build up a shared library of skills, you'll create a repository of microservices that can be repurposed and sequenced to achieve new goals. When your ecosystem reaches a point where AI and the members of your organization are working together seamlessly to create and evolve sequences that make up the ecosystem, you will have made hyperautomation into a team sport. Once you reach that state, you'll no longer be just automating the tasks that people used to perform—you'll be able to sequence technology to create new systems of automation.

So while the initial focus will be on automating specific tasks, the larger focus is on something a little more abstract. Pretend you wanted to automate the job of digging holes. Initially, you might build a robot that can wield a shovel and dig perfect holes at double a human's speed. That's fine automation. But what if, instead, you built a machine with 10 arms holding 10 shovels that could dig 10 holes at a time just as fast—and that is infinitely cloneable to boot. That's the spirit of hyperautomation.

Create an enterprise road map: Getting to that optimal state begins with treating the automation of immediate tasks as a vehicle for getting good and fast at solving complexity—and then keeping up momentum by iterating internally. This approach can get you deep into the process efficiently, especially if you create a road map. Even if it's incomplete and you change it every day, a road map will help set your sites on the skills you want to bring online for each new horizon that emerges.

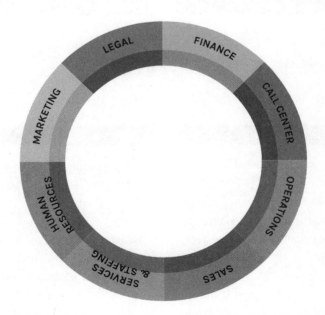

FIGURES 14.1 AND 14.2   *Some of the many functions within organizations where skills are being automated by companies today. (OneReach.ai)*

LEGAL

Contract-compliance (smart contracts)	Data collection & analysis
Contract-renewals	Contract management
Reminders	Manage workflow & flag errors in documents
Contract queries	
Q&A	

FINANCE

Pricing	Monitor & manage sales team-activity
Lead-input Communications	Scheduling
Analyze & predict sales data	

CALL CENTER

Scheduling	Outbound dialing
Customer communications	Call-backs
Data-collection & analysis	Sentiment-analysis
	Surveys
Advanced AI-driven IVR/ITR	Work Flow
	Remote management of phones & data

OPERATIONS

Data Analyses	Answer phones/automated conversations
Expense-tracking	
Communications	Data collection & analysis
Reminders	
Operations-tasks	Number-masking

SALES

Pricing	Analyze & predict sales data
Lead-input	Monitor & manage sales team-activity
Communications	
Scheduling	

SERVICES & STAFFING

Customer communication	Logistics-coordination & service-delivery
Data collection & analysis	Time-tracking
Scheduling	Q&A

HUMAN RESOURCES

Recruiter bot	Employee relocation-guide
Candidate-screening	On boarding/training
Time-tracking	Benefits enrollment
Employee satisfaction survey	Employee assessment
Reminders	Vacation/PTO
Employee handbook	
FAQ	

MARKETING

Encourage sign-ups	Low-cost SMS & email
Reminders	Website bot
Marketing management workflow	Surveys
Customer communications	Analyze marketing data & execute programs
Customer segmentation & analysis	Monitor social & alert and/or respond
	Q&A

FIGURES 14.1 AND 14.2 *(Continued)*

Scan to view the current version on your screen and for more use cases.

While Figure 14.3 might not look like one at first glance, this is an example road map of sorts, depicting the skills an organization may aspire to create, evolve, and expand upon. The colors of each tile, or skill, correspond to the different evolutionary stages, and the skills grow in complexity as they branch out from the starting point in the lower left corner.

When you flip back to the chapter on tools and architecture and look at this diagram from another angle (see Figure 11.3) it becomes clearer how, as we move along our journey, we ascend from basic skills toward more complex skills, each of which has its own evolutionary journey in a growing ecosystem.

Miss the Markov

The Markov chain is a popular design tool for good reason. (See Figure 14.4.) It's incredibly useful for building and optimizing technical architecture, as it illustrates the sequence of possible events in which the probability of each event depends only on the state attained in the previous event. The assumption is that you don't need any historical information to predict the future state if you know your present state. In conversational design, a Markov chain quickly becomes a Markov mess, as there is far too much variability in what the present state might be; plus, an ecosystem designed for hyperautomating can leverage all kinds of historical data—especially with return users—to try to determine what their present state might be. (See Figure 14.5.)

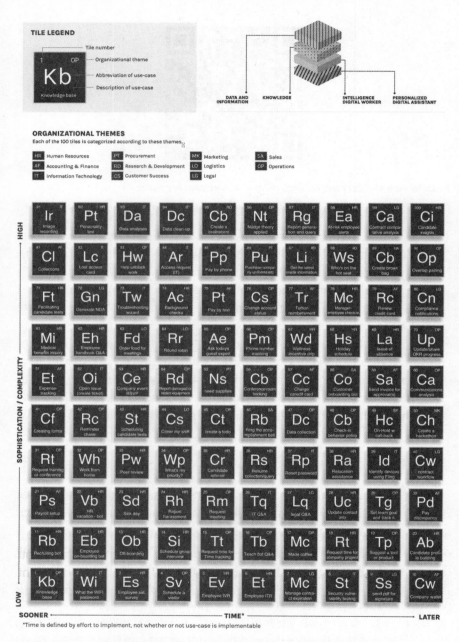

FIGURE 14.3   *Plotting aspirational hyperautomated skills.*

Scan to view this on your screen and for more examples.

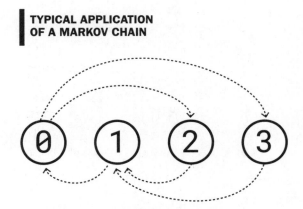

FIGURE 14.4   *Typical application of a Markov chain.*

Markov diagrams are a decent way to diagram multiple conversations in one diagram, but that diagramming isn't terribly helpful unless the problem you're trying to solve is how to articulate multiple conversation paths in one diagram. The flow of a conversation is linear, and there's a high degree of variation to the forms any one conversation can take. You don't know precisely where they will go, and in many scenarios you might not even know what the first point in an interaction will look like. Leaning on a Markov chain, you're more likely to end up with repetitive greetings and the wrong questions being asked. The alternative is a familiar tool of experience designers—the journey map.

MARKOV CHAIN MODEL ISN'T SUITABLE FOR CONVERSATIONAL DESIGN

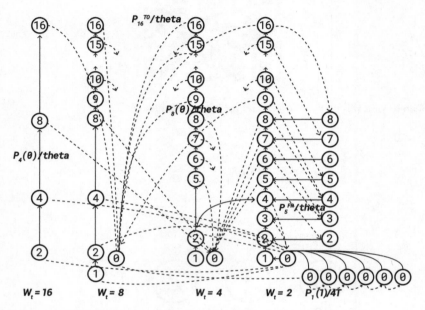

FIGURE 14.5   *Attempting to map multiple conversations using a Markov chain gets very messy.*

Map Your Journey

Journey maps illustrate a user's step-by-step journey through an experience. These maps are valuable for their ability to help stakeholders visualize something abstract, but in a typical UX setting they're often just a springboard toward design. In the realm of hyperautomation, journey maps are a crucial tool throughout the life cycle of a skill. They serve as both the shared vision of the team leading your automation efforts and thereafter become the initial reference point and vehicle for communicating future iterations. Journey maps are very much an active and direct reflection of the skills at play in your ecosystem.

Once you identify a skill you'd like to automate, you begin mapping the journey someone would have when engaging the automation. As is the case with all efforts in hyperautomating, your automation should always strive to outperform what a human alone would be capable of.

For instance, if you want to automate expense tracking, you'll want a deep familiarity with the current, human-run process so that you can map a new experience that eliminates redundancies, alleviates pain points, and runs more efficiently.

It's also essential to track a user's emotional state as they move through the steps and entry/exit points. As you build your user's journey, try to predict how they would be feeling based on their use case. For example, a user would likely be frustrated if they received a collection notice for a bill they already paid, so a conversation designed to resolve the issue should engage appropriately. In this case, the tone of the IDW should be direct and proactive, something along the lines of, "I apologize for the confusion and will work with you to get this resolved as quickly as possible."

As you test and deploy skills, you will gain deeper insights into the emotional states of users as they move through experiences. Users are frequently panicked when calling about a collection notice, which creates new opportunities to refine interactions. As you study and improve skills, you'll also become familiar with the many deviations a journey can take. Even with relatively straightforward skills, there can easily be multiple points along a single user's journey that will take them off the golden path and into a sub-journey. For example, in the same topic but for a different use case: "It looks like that collection notice was sent because the credit card associated with your account has expired. We sent multiple emails before issuing a collection notice. Would you like to <pay your outstanding balance> or <update your contact info>?"

As these alternate journeys emerge, they become part of your journey mapping as well. In your attempts to predict human behavior, remember that designers often design experiences for fake users who resemble rational actors—whereas, in reality, people can be very irrational.

USER: I don't want to pay this bill.
IDW: Are you sure? I can waive the late fee for you.
USER: Well, I won't pay.
IDW: Are you sure? This bill has been sent to collections, and paying it now will save you time and money.
USER: I'm not paying you anything.

Designing for irrational actors requires a system to reach levels of near general intelligence. The near-term workaround is to have machine-led conversations that bring humans into the loop to solve these unusual problems—while teaching the IDW how to handle similar situations on its own in the future.

As iterations improve outcomes and evolve skills, the journey map continues to sync with the skills in your ecosystem. Considering the scope and complexity of hyperautomation, these journey maps can become quite dense and interconnected and will serve as a lifeline. They are actually maps in a literal sense—you will need them to navigate and iterate on the growing number of skills within your ecosystem.

Skills are created using code-free tools and can be updated by virtually anyone in your organization using the journey maps to locate the steps that need to be revised. Initially, updates to the skills in your ecosystem will run through the core enablement team we explored previously. They are responsible for maintaining the integrity of your journey maps, and they will work alongside anyone in your organization who wants to either create a skill or evolve an existing one.

Commit to co-creating: I said earlier that variety can solve complexity. This is absolutely the case with hyperautomation. Looking at complex problems from a variety of perspectives is essential to solving them, and this means enlisting multiple people with diverse perspectives, experiences, and biases to work together. A core team of automation experts enabling other members of your organization to craft automations that meet their needs is the embodiment of solving complexity with variety.

Working with hyperautomation and conversational AI is a team sport. The members of your team have unique worldviews, skill sets, and technical aptitudes. Bringing those things together adds immeasurable richness to the automations you design. If your tools limit creation of these experiences to only those who can code, or if creation is shackled to your vendor's roadmap, then you're not going to be able to take advantage of the rich tapestry of knowledge and experience your team brings to the table. An open platform accelerates your entire team's ability to leverage disruptive technology.

This wondrous team sport of creating automated solutions starts with a workshop where you tease out a thorough understanding of the problem and define key success metrics. Following that, you'll want to hold development sessions with your internal business experts and the core enablement team diving deep on what's being automated. As solutions emerge and are tested and iterated on, communication stays strong, with members of the core enablement team keeping the momentum up and facilitating needs that arise. Processes will change rapidly, requiring quick iteration of automated skills, but that's not a problem, because your core enablement team is working in the trenches every day, evangelizing their shared vision.

Designing and training an IDW with a single skill, for instance, employee onboarding, is highly complex and dynamic given the amount of possible context. Which office will the new employee be working in? What position were they hired for? Do they have a disability? Training an IDW to complete this multi-turn task and evolving it to perform the task more efficiently requires attention from a human who knows the role they are trying to automate along with guidance from those who understand the ecosystem this IDW will inhabit and contribute to.

Projects and timelines are secondary as enablement goals become the primary objectives of this co-creating cohort. Organizations that are wired to fund projects based on measurable, quarterly ROI often face pressure to train and automate tasks concurrently. Here, co-creation is a valuable strategy—not only are you able to train, but by doing it with real-world problems you are able to more easily get buy-in from stakeholders.

You may or may not already have a conversational AI team. If you do, in this model they can find liberation from being sole creators (and potential bottlenecks), becoming consultative thought leaders, enablers, and evangelists for hyperautomating your organization. Establishing the type of core conversational team outlined in the next section and enabling them to co-create with your workforce will help to accelerate training and development of complex automation. This will set you up to solve complexity with variety, creating a new paradigm for every evolving automation within your organization, automation that simplifies operations as it grows more sophisticated.

As John Miller and Scott Page note in their book *Complex Adaptive Systems,* "Perhaps it is the case that, as we increase heterogeneity, we move from simple systems to complicated ones back to simple ones."[1]

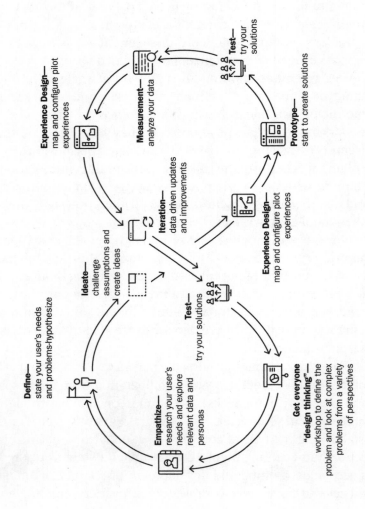

CO-CREATION PROCESS AT A GLANCE

Define— state your user's needs and problems-hypothesize

Ideate— challenge assumptions and create ideas

Experience Design— map and configure pilot experiences

Measurement— analyze your data

Test— try your solutions

Iteration— data driven updates and improvements

Prototype— start to create solutions

Experience Design— map and configure pilot experiences

Test— try your solutions

Get everyone "design thinking"— workshop to define the problem and look at complex problems from a variety of perspectives

Empathize— research your user's needs and explore relevant data and personas

FIGURE 14.6   *Co-creation process at a glance. (OneReach.ai)*

Scan to see how the process has evolved and more on this topic.

Build with human-in-the-loop: Creating great conversational experiences isn't easy; as a result, most of them are less than impressive. To avoid lackluster results, incorporate human-in-the-loop (HitL). With this approach, when a conversational application gets stuck, it can bring a human in to help. That human can ensure the end-user experience is fulfilled while also training the system so future occurrences don't require intervention. This type of training can either be done in real time, with algorithms to ensure the integrity of the training data, or through a

FIGURE 14.7 *Building with human-in-the-loop.*

moderation process where training is reviewed before it's applied. HitL requires an interface that is seamlessly integrated for real-time interactions and tools to match. For better or worse, the hype surrounding conversational AI has set end-user expectations high. HitL can help you meet those expectations in a timely manner that matches user needs.

Build and expand your shared library: There's no need to reinvent the wheel; instead, build and expand a shared library. A shared library is pivotal for co-creation, supplying your organization with an open resource of skills, services, and micro-services that can be reconfigured and resequenced across departments. It allows you to grow knowledge sharing and accelerate development while keeping control of security, compliance, monitoring, best practices, consistency, and scalability. Everyone in your organization can contribute to and draw from the shared library, making it the most scalable and effective way to move your organization into hyperautomation.

Leveraging the collective knowledge of your employees in this way can be game changing. When IDWs are designed to evolve and gain wisdom, not only can they have regular conversations with all of your employees and customers, you can also apply what you learn in real time.

Entering into this realm of complexity represents the dawning of a daunting journey, but with the right process, it becomes manageable. Former Hewlett Packard CEO Lee Platt once said, "If only HP knew what HP knows, we would be three times more productive." He may have vastly underestimated the increase in productivity but his point is clear: the knowledge is already there, it's your job to connect and activate the data.

Explore or exploit? It's the age-old question of diminishing returns—knowing when to continue searching for better solutions and when to start extracting value from what you've got can mark the difference between success and failure. The continuous improvement integral to hyperautomating requires striking a balance between explore and exploit.

A multitude of theories and algorithms have been leveraged to help locate the tipping point of explore/exploit, and it's been the subject of studies in psychiatry, behavioral ecology, computational neuroscience, computer science, and business.

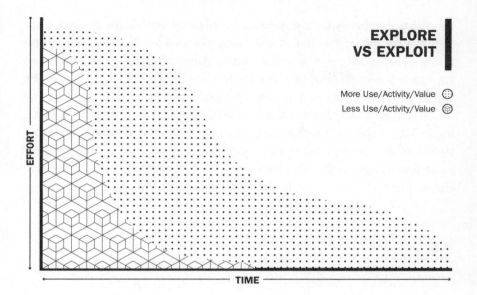

FIGURE 14.8 *Explore vs. exploit.*

The explore/exploit trade-off conundrum gets a little stickier in the realm of hyperautomation in that, as your organization smooths the rough edges of its ecosystem, you're always exploring. With the right process and tools in place, you'll be able to iterate quickly on solutions, making the balance of exploration and exploitation a more fluid process, with a faster cadence.

Pioneers in the realm of hyperautomation don't often have the opportunity to survey a wide variety of peers: other organizations in the hyperautomation trenches. Not only are there few great examples, but any examples (great or not) are highly competitive cards held extremely closely to the chest. What you can use to your advantage, however, is your ecosystem itself.

Ideally you'll have lots of people across your organization continually trying out new solutions, putting you in a better position to conduct lots of exploration, and discovering many solutions that bear fruit.

With accessible no-code tools for creating and analyzing solutions, iterating is faster and easier for teams. This collaborative approach can also foster success in spotting trends in what works well so that your exploits can bear ample fruit.

All said, the explore-exploit conundrum doesn't go away even as you're able, ready, and in the full swing of rapid creation, iteration, and analysis of solutions. You will still find yourself questioning, "How do we know when to continue improving our solution, and when is the right time to exploit the solution we have?"

There are many fascinating philosophies and some useful theories, formulas, and algorithms for trying to answer this question. My experience with creating and analyzing over 10,000 conversational applications has taught us to value two factors in particular that tend to drive the length or effort for exploring: volume and value.

Key Takeaways

- This isn't a software design scenario with weekly or monthly product milestones; this process allows you to experiment on active skills, continuously improving them while also activating new skills, multiple times, every day.

- As my team at OneReach.ai likes to say, "AI is a team sport"— one that requires collaboration across every department within an organization, with ideas for improving skills coming in from every direction.

- A successful strategy for hyperautomation starts small and internally, with everyone in your workforce leveraging their individual areas of expertise to develop and evolve skills.

- Journey maps of experiences users will have with your automations will serve as the shared vision for your team and the initial reference point and vehicle for communicating future iterations.

- Continuous building with human-in-the-loop and expanding your shared library are critical pieces of a sound strategy for hyperautomation.

- The continuous improvement integral to hyperautomating requires striking a balance between explore and exploit, but that balance can be achieved with more fluidity as you iterate quickly on solutions.

Visit Invisiblemachines.ai for more information on the process evolving technical aspects of hyperautomation.

CHAPTER 15

Design Strategy for Hyperautomation

I've noted how conversation is the most natural way for humans to connect with one another and accomplish shared goals. Even though communicating conversationally is second nature to most people, designing conversational experiences isn't as easy as you might expect. In a regular one-on-one conversation with another human, you say something and get immediate feedback, whether it's verbal, non-verbal, or both, That feedback tells you what to do or say next. When designing a conversation for an IDW, you're tasked with creating one side of an interaction and making your best guesses as to what the likely responses might include. It can be extremely difficult to do this well, but you get better at figuring out the best ways to design interactions by moving through the create-test-improve loop at a rapid pace.

It's a bit like generating new material as a comedian. You can come up with jokes you think are good, but you won't know if they're funny or not until you test them on live audiences. The key difference is that, once the best jokes are identified and honed, the comedian's work on them is done for the most part. The material is presented in a one-sided format, and the only follow-up to consider is the next joke. But conversational design is two-sided, and so these interactions can take many different turns based on the different ways different users reply. Each subsequent turn might lead to a new set of choices, so the complexity compounds in a hurry.

The key to staying on track is keeping practical conversations at the core of your strategy. People are turning to you for help, so be helpful. This approach will also help you avoid the most common failure point: lack of end-user adoption. Like a joke that never gets a laugh, all your efforts are for nothing if people don't use what you build. Bear in mind as well that, to a user, the interface *is* the system. This is true in most design scenarios involving technology, but it becomes exceedingly important when dealing with conversational interfaces. The more high functioning a conversational AI experience is, the more intuitive it will feel for users to interact with it—and the more readily they will accept it as "the system." However, a conversational interface only achieves that kind of potent simplicity when it's properly architected behind the scenes.

The conversational interface—whether it's expressed as an IDW, chatbot, or virtual agent—is just a construct. The intelligence and sophistication of the interface aren't determined by the interface itself; it's an active reflection of the sum of all parts of the ecosystem. Much of this high-level design strategy work falls to your lead experience architect (LXA), who is building something akin to wireframe in web design. Armed with patterns that create rewarding conversational experiences for users, the LXA can assemble the bones of countless automations.

With conversational AI, users aren't comparing their experience with your solution to experiences with other similar technologies; they're comparing them to experiences they have in conversation with other humans. But as we've noted, the designer's job isn't to mimic human interactions—it's to go far beyond human interactions. The real value comes from sequencing technologies to design experiences that are improvements on current workflows. This differs from what many experience designers are aiming for. In the realm of GUIs, good design is unobtrusive and reduces friction. While these are goals in conversational design as well, the overarching goal is to create experiences that contribute to a much larger environment and web of experiences.

Design for Human-Controlled Outcomes

Technology should make us happy. From an experience design perspective, all tools are, in essence, forms of technology, and the successful ones improve our lives. In fact, this implies it's crucial that hyperautomated experiences are designed to keep decision-making in human hands.

Why? Because humans are only happy when they feel like they have options. According to psychologist (and popular *UX Magazine* contributor) Susan Weinschenk, PhD, "Given an easy way to accomplish a task, versus a way that just makes our life more difficult, why do we sometimes (often?) choose the way that is complicated? It's because we love having control."[1]

Having choices gives people a sense of control, and people are drawn to a bevy of choices. Starbucks brags that their cafés offer more than 170,000 ways to customize beverages. Their reasoning behind this arch; flexibility? So "customers can create a favorite drink that fits their lifestyle."[2] Some of the more extreme examples of drinks that fit customer lifestyles have gone viral on social media, such as a venti Caramel Ribbon Crunch Frappuccino with 13 additions, "including extra ice, five 'banana,' and seven pumps of dark caramel sauce."[3] Whether this strikes you as delicious or excessive, it's interesting to think what might happen when people can use conversational interfaces to focus creative energies brought on by a thirst for better choices on designing software solutions that fit their lifestyle.

Through hyperautomation, we can improve the quality of the choices people make, imbuing them with meaning and impact. We do this by designing for human-controlled outcomes (HCO). Nobody wants to wake up under strict orders from a machine to be told what to do all day by machines designed to maximize their efficiency. On the other hand, people will love interacting conversationally with machines that offer them informed choices throughout the day that will increase their efficiency. Hyperautomation needs to be human-led at every level. Even if a machine is capable of making decisions on its own—and perhaps even more efficiently than a human can—good design keeps humans in the driver's seat. For example, even though modern commercial airliners can take off, fly, and land by themselves, a human can always take control whenever they want to. By design, the barrage of technologies working in concert to fly a commercial airliner exist to help the humans in the cockpit make better piloting decisions.

A sound design strategy for conversational AI within an intelligent ecosystem of digital workers relies on many service patterns that are practical and hew to similar interactions with another human. These patterns also represent opportunities to evolve processes and create truly innovative automations. The one pattern that should guide them all, however, is keeping decision-making in human hands. Find ways to help people make more meaningful and consequential decisions, and you will make people happier and more productive. In some ways it's just that simple.

Sequencing Patterns for a Successful Ecosystem

Successful automations call for successfully sequenced patterns. Within the kind of ecosystems I've been describing, those patterns inevitably invite a great deal of complexity. A great frame of reference for this concept is the game of chess, which is all about recognizing and acting on complex patterns.

"Pattern recognition is one of the most important mechanisms of chess improvement," International Master Arthur van de Oudeweetering wrote. "Realizing that the position on the board has similarities to positions you have seen before helps you to quickly grasp the essence of that position and find the most promising continuation."[4]

By some estimates, grandmasters of chess can memorize up to 100,000 patterns. While this is an impressive feat, putting memorized patterns to use isn't really what humans are wired to do. At some point people make mistakes while acting on patterns, no matter how ingrained they are. It stands to reason that I should be able to enter the passcode on my alarm system flawlessly, every time. I've had plenty of practice, but sometimes I mess up and have to start over again. There's always going to be uncertainty when people are in charge of patterns. In a podcast interview with Lex Fridman, rapper, record producer, philosopher, chess player, and mastermind of the Wu-Tang Clan, RZA, sheds light on the idea of uncertainty:

"[With chess] the thing that's introduced is the uncertainty . . . you gonna make a move [and] sooner or later something uncertain is going to come in. . . . Bobby Fisher said in one of his books, 'Every game of chess is a draw, the only way somebody wins is when one of us makes a mistake.'"[5] Grandmaster Savielly Tartakower echoes this notion:

"The winner of the game is the player who makes the next-to-last mistake." When it comes to recognizing patterns and acting on them without making mistakes, machines have a decided edge over humans.

Back in 1997, chess grandmaster Garry Kasparov resigned after 19 moves in a game against a chess-playing computer developed by IBM called Big Blue. It was the sixth and final game of their match, and Kasparov lost two games to one, with three draws. In 2010, Kasparov wrote, "Today, for $50, you can buy a home PC program that will crush most grandmasters." While the fact that machines are better at chess than humans might be unwelcome news to grandmasters, it's great for hyperautomating.

The reason computers beat humans at chess is that they can memorize 100,000 patterns and run through them with flawless recognition and total confidence. But rather than pitting human against machine, hyperautomation provides humans the opportunity to forge and sequence patterns that machines can then use to automate tasks without uncertainty. This isn't to say that these patterns will perform flawlessly right away—but as you continually improve upon them, you can reach a point where a growing number of tasks within your organization are performed with total certainty.

Getting to this place requires help from humans with something they are *better at* doing than machines are: predicting behavior. When someone poses a question, we use all sorts of cues (visual, physical, historical, auditory, etc.) to understand what's really being asked. If we don't immediately know how to respond with a helpful reply, we can make an educated guess based on the context. For example, let's say a coworker asks me if they look okay—and they look as though they haven't slept for days. We're about to go into an important meeting, so I don't think they're looking for an honest answer—and it definitely wouldn't help, so I decide to offer a platitude instead. On the other hand, if that person wanted feedback in advance on how to remove a stain of their shirt, an honest answer would be appropriate.

Before you touch any technology, however, you need to envision the experience you want to create. I've studied numerous highly rated experiences over the years and have noted scores of patterns that lead to good experiences, and we'll explore them in the next section. Keeping these patterns in mind as you build the framework of your ecosystem—designing automation flows and strategizing their deployment—can help create an ecosystem of real service. Not only can the sequencing of these patterns efficiently automate tasks with certainty, these are the kinds of optimized experiences that will build meaningful relationships between humans and machines. They should be designed as something ongoing that will evolve—not as a series of disconnected transactions but as contextual relationships. Thinking beyond transactional relationships to contextual relationships creates the opportunity to change the presence of software and machines in our lives so that technology can be always present but never invasive.

This work often begins with journey maps created by lead experience architects and design strategists. These journey maps are used to define the experiences that make up your ecosystem, and they come to life as key patterns are identified and later fleshed out through production design. Nothing about this process is one-and-done. Like the nearly infinite number of moves that could take place on a chessboard, there's really no limit to how patterns like these can be sequenced and continually improved. Another nugget of chess wisdom shared by RZA applies readily to hyperautomation:

> I recall the first time that I realized that I need to improve. At first I was probably the best player in the crew. But the crew started improving. I had to do more play[ing]. But . . . the GZA himself, he started studying [chess] theory, studying books I wasn't aware of. One day at his crib he was beating me so bad, and his son Kareem, who loves his big cousin Rakeem [RZA] . . . so he just came over when GZA went to the bathroom, he was like, "Yo, you know my dad is in the books, right?" [laughs hard].[6]

When you're hyperautomating, you should always be in the books—not only to keep an edge on competing businesses but also to continue to improve the more personalized relationships you can build with customers.

Now, let's take a closer look at the patterns your lead experience architects and design strategists will want to keep in their back pocket as you build your ecosystem for hyperautomation. We'll start with the most basic patterns and work toward the more complex ones.

Key Patterns to Sequence for Conversational AI

Question and answers: Q&A is one of the most basic conversational patterns, and it's what a lot of people mistakenly think of as conversational AI. Users ask the machine a question, and it looks for the answer using natural language understanding (NLU) and a knowledge base designed for providing answers. The Q&A pattern highlights one area where conversation isn't always the best solution: browsing. Q&A is a way to help resolve a question that the user has, but depending on your use case, giving them the option to browse data, products, or an FAQ page might be more useful. Adding a graphical UI in addition to the conversational UI can be a way to solve this. For example, if someone asks about what types of services are available, the IDW can point them to the page on the website that lists all of the services. In ecosystems built for hyperautomation, the IDW can also turn to a human-in-the-loop if it doesn't have an answer.

Find: Users ask the machine to look up information based on certain queries. The machine queries an API and gets a set of results that it can show the user. This might feedback into known answers for Q&A or help with transactions or establish the user's identity. Even though the Q&A and find patterns seem similar, they are very different. Find is a good pattern to employ if Q&A fails to help.

Since these design patterns come from pieces of successful human conversation, they are ultimately derived from human interaction. Like machines, we only have a certain amount of experience and training. When necessary, we use external sources such as the Internet, colleagues, and books to find the answers we need. In the context of find, when a machine's training doesn't allow it to answer the question, it can search external sources, usually via API.

Chase: Chase is more aggressive than simple reminders; flows built for this will activate continuously until a certain criterion is met. For example, a proactive pattern would hunt down an answer to a particular question. If a user doesn't provide it, the machine will move on to another user—or else continue to repeat the query until it gets its answer. Often, successful resolution will involve escalation.

Nudge: Nudge is a soft push toward a desired outcome but in a manner that's less intrusive than chase. It's designed to provide extra information in a structured way that will either subconsciously motivate users to take a particular action or more distinctly prompt them to consciously make the intended choice. A tangible example would be painted lines on a road that clearly delineate cyclists from drivers. The best uses are contextual to the experience they're in. In the airline industry, for example, a nudge might be: "Just so you know, an upgrade to business class for this flight is only $99 more."

Drip: Drip is a series of announcements; it can be used for reporting and making enhancements that don't require immediate feedback. It's a bit like chase without the knowledge base and providing future context. For example, drip would offer: "Don't forget, you have an appointment on Monday at 3:30 p.m.," whereas chase would offer: "Please confirm your appointment on Monday at 3:30 p.m. by replying, 'Y' or 'N.'" Drip often represents a content journey, one that's presented in a predetermined sequence. For example, a drip might have a series of five deliberately spaced out messages that go out to first-time customers as part of an onboarding experience with a new product.

Memorize: This pattern can also establish conversational patterns at large across multiple users. Memorize can be used to understand the common conversations and questions that users engage in. Flows built for memorization will store information so that it can be used for reporting, making enhancements to the knowledge base, and providing future context. When designing your conversations, you should make sure that you set them up to store data so that you can utilize memorize. Ultimately, this context helps to build relationships rather than just one-off transactions.

Remind: Remind is a proactive pattern that gives users information at a particular time and in a specific way in order to take action.

This could be for an upcoming appointment or to establish a new habit. In order to succeed with this very common pattern, send out reminders over whatever channel your customer prefers. In fact, this is another chance to employ the memorize pattern—noting preferred channels for engagement.

In most designs I've seen, remind is used mundanely—without much imagination—as a simple outbound message. Using only one pattern on its own doesn't make for a good conversation. To use remind successfully, design around the reminder and create a conversational experience that goes beyond the first obvious step.

Track: This is similar to memorize but isn't necessarily used for long-term memorization. For example, the machine might memorize how many times a user goes from point A to B, tracking that everything between point A to B is being logged and used. Flows that track are keeping in mind a "current state"—as well as all the prior states that led to that point.

Callback: Another proactive pattern, callback is focused on resuming a prior activity. This is geared toward pausing an activity and setting a follow-up—an interval that could be dependent on a certain amount of time lapsing or on the emergence of a new piece of data.

Contextualize: With contextualize, the machine is trying to extract context from the conversation using stored data as a starting point. It will query its contextual storage and try to continue from that context. Examples could include using time of day, location, the task at hand, or a prior conversation or message in order to establish context. The contextualize pattern is beneficial in that it allows the machine to use context to improve the conversational experience by cutting out the need for starting from the beginning—such as asking questions like "Are you a customer? When was your most recent purchase?" This pattern goes hand in hand with the memorize pattern.

Guide: With this pattern, the machine literally guides a user from point A to point B, such as in a scripted conversation or a sequence of questions. Guide could also help with a particular sequence over time, such as checking in each day to help users stay on track with a specific goal. Flows built to guide keep in mind progression and sequence with the milestones or the ultimate outcome they're meant to achieve. Guide is also a critical pattern for the concierge skill, which greets users. Concierge evaluates a user's needs using patterns such as contextualize and Q&A; then, it uses guide to connect users to the other skills in the ecosystem that will help them achieve their goals. Without guide, a user would be left guessing what an IDW might be capable of, asking questions that wouldn't help the system differentiate what they're *really* asking for.

Interactions that follow the user's lead can be complex and difficult to build, which can lead to a common mistake with conversational design: overpromising or letting users expect that your machine can do more than it actually can. Set expectations for your user by guiding them—rather than imposing on them to guide the machine.

Transact: This pattern helps users accomplish a particular task. There's a goal in mind and a desired outcome; common examples would be scheduling an appointment or ordering a product. Transact can also be used for minor changes to a setting or to add a new communication preference. Flows will have a structured script that needs particular information to complete the task, with task completion being the primary measure.

Negotiate: If someone asks an IDW if you can check into a hotel room early and it replies that check-in time is 4 p.m., they might be inclined to call and try and persuade someone to bend the rules their way. Trying to persuade a machine is futile, but you can prevent that phone call by building negotiation into the process. In this case, the IDW can negotiate by saying something like, "If our regular check-in time of 4 p.m. doesn't work for you, let me see if I can try and work something out and get back to you." This gives the user the impression that calling would be futile, so they'll wait to hear back from the IDW—likely employing HitL to get an answer.

Promises and assignments: This pattern was inspired by a concept that developers often use in JavaScript that has an asynchronous component to it: someone either promises to take care of a certain task the next time they log in or assigns someone else to take care of a task when they next log in. In most scenarios people tend to think of interactions with machines as being either inbound (someone is calling you) or outbound (you reach out or are responding to someone). Promises and assignments represents a third category, the real-life equivalent of which would be me telling you, "Hey, next time you talk to Teddy, remind him he owes me $100." Within an ecosystem for hyperautomating, this takes the form of a queue of assignments so that the next time Teddy contacts the organization, he receives these assignments. It's almost like an inbox that only reveals its queue of messages when someone makes inbound contact. You already see this pattern used by cell-phone companies: when you call, they remind you that you're due for a device upgrade. With inbound calls this pattern can be used to deftly avoid prolonged calls. For instance, if someone who recently placed an order calls in, there's an assignment at the top of their queue to let them know: "I see you ordered something from us earlier this week. Good news—your order has shipped! Would you like the tracking information?" A personalized experience like this saves the user time and engenders confidence in the IDW. Promises and assignments is an amazing pattern because it allows you to go further without annoying people. They've already reached out to you; meet them with some useful information that can save them time.

Coordinate: This pattern is meant to get several participants working together around a particular goal. This might be used to schedule a meeting or gather shared input. This is a more complex pattern that will often have sub-patterns such as chase, track, and transact working together.

Share: This pattern is designed to share information with people who need it. This proactive pattern helps disseminate information in a relevant or contextual way. Flows that use share will send out messages or links bearing useful information.

Teach: This pattern teaches users how to do something, often launching from Q&A. The purpose is to provide a series of lessons and/or instruction, which can occur in a single session or across multiple sessions.

Predict: With this pattern the machine uses past interactions and contextual data to predict what a user might be trying to do, often suggesting possible outcomes, such as by saying: "This option is statistically more likely to produce your desired outcome." By reviewing all available data to predict possible outcomes, predict eliminates unnecessary steps to make the conversation as efficient as possible.

Process mining: A machine can be trained to analyze data with the objective of identifying patterns, inefficiencies, and opportunities in both current and historical processes and events.

Anomaly detection: Anomaly detection is a process mining pattern for detecting anomalies in data, such as events or deviations from what is standard or expected.

Anomalous absence detection: An especially valuable type of anomaly detection involves regular evaluation of data with the particular goal of detecting something humans aren't typically good at spotting: the absence of data. Essentially, the machine identifies patterns and meaning in the absence of data, and treats each absence as an event—which in some cases could amount to identifying missed opportunities or opportunity costs.

For example, a human account manager might notice that a customer, JoAnna H, made a larger purchase than most customers make within a six-month period. But it's less likely that the same human would notice that JoAnna H had anomalously *not* bought anything in the same six-month period (absence of data), whereas an IDW could alert the account manager to Joanna H's buying drought so that the organization can reach out with a special offer for her next purchase.

Machine-in-the-middle: This is a relatively simple pattern that involves a live agent handing off a user to an IDW in order to perform a task that a machine can do more efficiently. For instance, if you've been talking to an agent to arrange specific details of a purchase, that agent can then hand you over to an IDW to collect payment information (maybe a text pops up on your phone requesting your credit card number or a photo of the back of your card). Another example: you email a service provider with a query, and an IDW tasked with reviewing emails sent to their support team detects missing information. You get a follow-up email from the IDW requesting your account number and the service address so that when the agent pulls up the ticket, all of the information is there. This unburdens the agent from having to do additional follow-ups and helps your request reach a faster resolution.

This is also an important pattern to keep in mind because it demonstrates that there are plenty of creative ways to build automations that don't require APIs or extensive integration. Machine-in-the-middle can simply be that an IDW that receives an inbound email uses NLU to see and review the content and determines whether there's missing information. The IDW can reply right away asking users for missing data—no integration necessary.

Human-in-the-loop (HitL): Automation is only as good as the data at its disposal. In this powerful pattern, humans provide data to help train the IDW—and there are endless conversations or variations of conversations that humans can help with. Flows that incorporate HitL reach out to their humans-in-the-loop on different channels—whether it's a call center, chat channels, text messages, or collaborative tools such as Slack—to get the needed information; in turn, the flows update their knowledge bases and skills. In other scenarios—as has been previously covered—when the IDWs get stuck on a problem, they are guided by humans with what to do next. Team members can either feed the IDW information for machine learning or script their interactions in a particular way.

Human-controlled outcomes (HCO): Hyperautomation needs to be human-led at every level. Machines' abilities to make efficient decisions on their own will continue to improve, but it's crucial to keep people in control of outcomes. People don't want to live under strict orders from machines—even if those machines are designed to maximize efficiency. But people will likely look forward to interacting with machines that regularly offer efficiency-improving suggestions.

Metacognitive behavior: This is more of an overarching pattern—one that embraces and reinforces many of those described above. The idea is to create a pattern of awareness within your ecosystem so that, while IDWs are learning individual skills, they are also managing their overall learning. It's one thing to learn a skill—dogs, for instance, do it all the time—but it's another thing to be actively aware that you are learning (and to subsequently project-manage that learning). For our purposes, this could be as basic as having an IDW check in about learning a new skill set along a timeline. It could also include higher-level functionalities, like having an IDW check in with suggestions based on user queries (e.g. "I've noticed many users are calling to request password resets. Is this something I can learn to do?"). You could also seek out new tools for your ecosystem and then vet them based on reputation or user ratings.

KEY DESIGN PATTERNS

For Lead Experience Architects and Design Strategists To Keep In Their Back Pocket

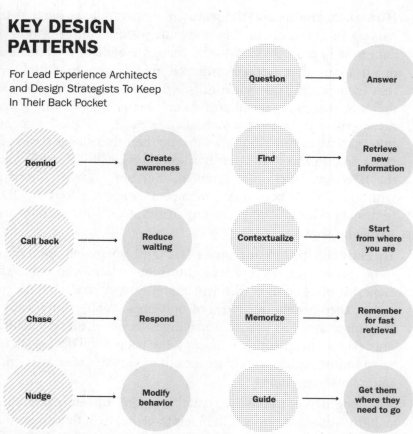

FIGURES 15.1 AND 15.2 *Key design patterns to sequence for conversational design. (OneReach.ai)*

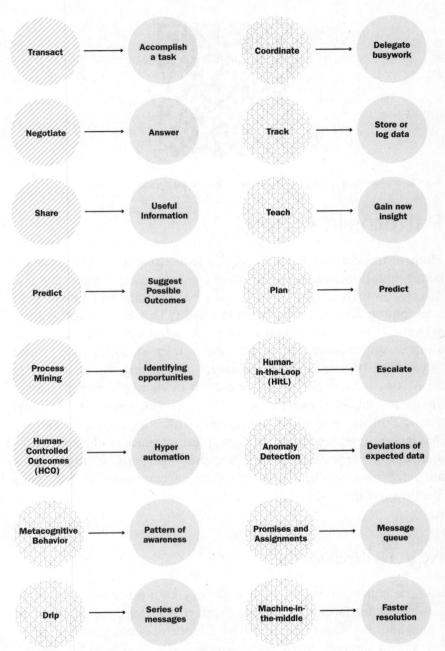

FIGURES 15.1 AND 15.2   *(Continued)*

Scan to explore these and growing explorations of patterns.

Patterns in Action

Many of these patterns are frequently sequenced by GPS to provide a better-than-human experience. You've got some extra time as you're driving through an unfamiliar area to a meeting, so you ask your smartphone if there's a coffee shop nearby. This is the **Q&A** pattern activated. The answer might come back in the form of pinpoints on a map, using the **contextualize** pattern to find a coffee shop closest to you. The system can then **guide** you, navigating you to the coffee shop. It can also use the **predict** pattern to identify a traffic accident up ahead that could cause a delay. It can **nudge** you to let you know that you might want to take a side street. This is a multimodal journey that incorporates voice, text, and graphical interface, and it can evolve to include other patterns, such as **transact**—perhaps letting you order and pay for your coffee ahead of time, so you can be sure to make your meeting on time.

Key Takeaways

- The conversations we have every day with other people provide instant feedback that informs the flow, whereas designing conversations involves starting with a prompt and taking your best guess at how someone might reply.
- People are turning to you for help, so be helpful by keeping practical conversations at the core of your strategy and avoid the most common failure point: low user adoption.

- Successful automations are built by sequencing design patterns— which machines are good at running flawlessly—using your advanced human ability to predict behavior as a guide.
- Sequencing of the patterns recommended here can create optimized experiences that will build meaningful relationships between humans and machines.
- Patterns can make your bot more helpful, to take your bot from being an underachiever to being an overachiever.

Visit Invisiblemachines.ai for more information on design strategy in the realm of hyperautomation.

CHAPTER 16

Production Design for Hyperautomation

The notion of having real conversations with computers has been the stuff of science fiction until relatively recently. It took decades, but speech recognition has improved to a place of near human recognition, which, incidentally, is not as great as most might think. Simply translating sounds into words does not constitute understanding. Understanding comes with comprehension of what the words mean and what the user intends by speaking them. Whether you're dealing specifically with speech or with other communication channels, this is where production design comes in.

In this space, production design consists of a conversational designer creating the experiences people will have in conversations with machines. In terms of more traditional experience design it's analogous to a designer skinning a wireframe. The lead experience architect maps out the high-level journey users will take with an IDW. Now, the conversational designer creates the flows that facilitate that high-level journey, choosing words and fine-tuning the tone to bring the experience to life.

As far as users are concerned, the conversational interface *is* the system. This is a good thing.

But it's critical that designers and architects not confuse the interface for the system on *their* end.

You might be surprised at how quickly you can find yourself empathizing with a conversational interface—and this is a testament to the ingrained nature of conversation as a tool. But since the conversational interface is just the access point, the success of NLU hinges on whether it understands language and context deeply enough to determine the user's intention. That contextual understanding is forged by a properly designed ecosystem. So as you fine-tune your conversational design, always bear in mind that it's not the system— it's the portal *into* the system.

The remains of many a concierge bot can be found in the ruins of failed attempts at implementing conversational AI. This happens when a machine with no actual skill—even one that's running on a sophisticated NLU engine—is propped up as being the one-stop portal into an organization. If users aren't informed of what a machine can do, they might think the machine can do anything, which of course isn't possible. As I indicated when describing the guide pattern in the previous chapter, concierge isn't a machine; it's a skill, and it's usually the first skill a user will encounter. The concierge skill evaluates a user's needs by asking questions that can map to other skills in the ecosystem. The concierge skill determines which skills will most likely be of benefit and connects the user to them. (For example, if it's dealing with a return visitor, an IDW running the concierge skill can cross-reference existing customer data during the initial interaction to get a head start on a useful reply.) Once the IDW has an idea of what the user wants, using whatever NLU engine best suits the use case, it can guide the user between skills so as to deliver a rewarding, better-than-human experience.

Everything Hinges on Analytics and Reporting

You may not be surprised to hear that hyperautomating requires a completely new relationship with analytics and tracking. There's a side to this new relationship that will be thrilling and revelatory, for hyperautomating requires tools that let you analyze and report on interactions between users and IDWs in real time. In essence this creates a powerful and integrated form of user research. Of course, something this novel and high yield requires an ecosystem with deeply elaborate architecture.

With the implementation of conversational AI, analytics and reporting are inseparable—providing information crucial to the establishment and evolution of your ecosystem—but they operate somewhat independently within that ecosystem. Even the most basic user experiences with conversational AI produce massive amounts of data, which is a good thing from an analytics perspective: the more information, the better. But conversation interfaces yield unstructured data that requires analytics to give it shape and meaning. Combine that swelling pool of nebulous information with an organization's internal data—specifically, the data that's feeding the conversational experience—and you're facing some profound complexity.

It's also worth pausing on connected devices because the Internet of things that don't look like computers but act like computers are data points as well. Whether we recognize it as such or not, we spend our lives surrounded by computers of all shapes and sizes. If your refrigerator recognizes that its door is being opened and starts running software, the door has become an interface, and the appliance is as much a computer as it is a cooling unit. So add all the data cached by televisions, speakers, Bluetooth tags, and cat litter boxes to your collection of data sources to be reckoned with.

If you're an analyst, data is your friend. Let's say you've got a hypothesis to test and want to explore as much data as possible—running it through different filters looking for patterns. There are various tools out there, such as machine learning, that let you crunch large amounts of data and find actionable patterns to exploit. For hyperautomation efforts, these tools don't need to work in real time, but they need to be flexible so that analysts can explore data in many ways.

Let's say you're an analyst for a subscription-based cat litter company. You have a hunch that when customers move they often cancel their subscriptions and restart them again later rather than just updating their address information. You run the data to see if that correlation is supported. You find a pattern of users who have cancelled subscriptions and then created new ones with different addresses. This is valuable, actionable information that you then pass along to an experience designer.

When XDs are building conversational workflows for IDWs, they can implement algorithms built around the patterns provided by analysts. In our kitty litter scenario, the XD could add prompts when users first sign on and when they initiate a cancellation. The XD can design ways to communicate to users that updating their address is easy—easier than cancelling and then starting up again.

As they make these kinds of adjustments, XDs can use real-time reporting to learn what's working and what isn't. In some cases, they might even improve interactions as they're happening. This is the nature of reporting in hyperautomation scenarios. Reporting is always on and always being acted on. Tactically speaking, this requires a dashboard that allows experience designers to watch as users interact with IDWs, moving through a series of skills and flows. When experience designers can literally see how users are interacting with machines, they can be regularly fine-tuning interactions.

The data supply that comes with most of the machines that people release into the wild are black boxes with basic metrics (attrition, hang-ups, etc.) and are of little use when creating an ecosystem for hyperautomation. Unless you're summarizing data in real time, you'll find it exceedingly hard to patch holes in your boat before the water pours in. Being able to retrace conversations in a timely fashion is the real value and the real-time reporting aspect needs to be baked into whatever tool you're using.

What's required is an ever-spinning feedback loop. As skills are deployed and utilized, those interactions can be analyzed and iterated on, often as they unfold. This isn't a nice-to-have, it's an imperative. If you can't easily report on how people are using your system and experiences, you'll find it impossible to fulfill the promise of rapid iteration, which is critical for hyperautomation. Hyperautomation allows us to create hyperpersonalized solutions, but that hyperpersonalization requires this deeper, ingrained relationship with analytics and reporting.

Not only is this the most efficient way to aggregate and actualize vast amounts of data within your ecosystem, it's also a boon to your team. In this scenario, data analysts get to focus squarely on what they do best: digging through data and identifying patterns. In complementary fashion, your experience designers will be designing experiences that are truly dynamic, relying on an exciting new rate of iteration that should ignite the creative spirit of anyone passionate about the progression of experience design as a discipline.

In some ways, this is a dynamic new form of experience design that represents the process in its purest form. By designing experiences, watching them unfold in real time, and taking opportunities to continually improve on them, you're flowing through steps hourly or daily that would be weeks or even months apart in typical software development scenarios. This creates a feedback loop that lets you design and maintain incredibly powerful software at a rapid pace.

Keep in mind, however, that companies are not successful because they produce more software but because they produce more good software. This is where this new approach to experience design pays off. When experience designers no longer have to concern themselves with being developers—when they can create and evolve software at will without having to write code—they can focus squarely on designing truly good software.

Strive for Adaptative Design

Adaptive design is a next-level concept that involves a rapid iteration loop of testing, analyzing, and designing. The idea is that by testing a variety of combinations of things, you'll gain valuable insights that you can design around. My team assisted Stanford University as part of a study that used text messaging to help parents teach kids to read. The entire objective was to find the right combination of content, language, and scheduling to get the most positive effect. What we discovered was that this kind of communication can be very powerful in terms of modifying human behavior—so long as it's continuously fine-tuned to maximize the effect.

For example, just because a text prompt asking a parent to have their child read a line from a cereal box works at 7:30 a.m. for the first four weeks doesn't mean it will remain effective forever. The UI needs to adapt by running through the cycle of explore vs. exploit: exploring the right combo to optimize the experience, then exploiting it until it wanes, and then going back to explore.

Different patterns also work differently for different people or personas. You have to be able to adapt on a schedule but also from a standpoint of individualization. My team applied this thinking to a service-finding service, such as homeowners needing work to be done. Of course, if the first time someone tried to use the service no provider showed up, they'd never use the service again, so it's critical that the first interaction go well. We were able to ensure that the providers show up on time (and also that the homeowner was there to meet them) by exploring numerous combinations based on language, time, and reminders. We allowed the system to adapt to things such as alert fatigue and leveraged all of the individual data we could identify. (For example, roofers might respond to a site visit request differently than plumbers would, since they need more advance notice to prepare materials.)

Phrasing and timing can be customized on an individual basis. Being able to adapt an optimized formula and realizing it can be optimized again helps you create an environment for machine learning—where there is no perfect combo because nothing is static. It sounds like a lot of work, but the power and effect make it worth every minute. When it comes together, the ability to modify behavior is unbelievable. I know how powerful this approach can be because we've used it to effectively help people quit smoking—one of the most powerful addictions to break.

Some things are complex for the sake of complexity. This is complexity that brings about the power of personalization.

New Door, Same Old LATCH

Even though the analytics and reporting paradigm I'm describing here is novel, there's an empirical method of categorizing data that's as useful as ever: LATCH. According to Robert Saul Wurman, the creator of LATCH (and founder of TED), "I believe, and it has been accepted, that there are only five ways of organizing information. I use the acronym LATCH: Location, alphabet, time, category, and hierarchy."[1] These five categories can be applied to all types of information and can be particularly useful when dealing with the volume of information that needs sorting inside an ecosystem built for hyperautomating. Wurman described how it works in a press video for his book *Information Anxiety 2*:

> *If I threw 120,000 words on the floor, you wouldn't call it a dictionary. But, if you organize them alphabetically, you call it a dictionary. Now if I [organize] them in groups and those groups have meaning . . . you call it an encyclopedia. . . . [If] we can organize [them] . . . by time, then it would be a book on history. We could organize them by location and it would be an atlas. We can organize them by the biggest to the smallest or smallest to largest and we'd have our list of tens. Like . . . whatever that guy David Letterman does. [2]*

Thinking about the different ways to classify and render data using LATCH can inform how you guide analytics and design your reports.

Best Practices in Analytics and Reporting

Here are some of the best practices to follow when leveraging analytics and reporting within your ecosystem.

Use tracking points for skills-based path reporting: Tracking your IDW's performance requires close attention to metrics such as task completion (what did users accomplish with your IDW?) and golden paths (pathways that are most commonly used, and should be prioritized for optimal experience). Keep in mind that users hanging up on or abandoning IDWs are sometimes golden paths if the user left because they got the info they needed.

Using tracking points to measure the paths people take through skills and conversations, your goal is to identify golden paths; failed paths ending in ways that are not designed; incomplete paths, which are not finished but that users intend to finish;

and missing paths, which are not handled by the system but that users are looking for.

You should always be ready to address exceptions such as time-outs and error logs. When tagging flows, remember that a user may complete multiple skills in a single conversation. Conversation outcomes might include several skills and may be initiated by an IDW and ended by a user. Logging the average time spent in a conversation is often less useful globally, but it is helpful at the skill level.

These outcomes are helpful to consider as you design:

- Contained: conversations that were contained and didn't require human intervention;
- HitL: either requested by IDW or human intervention was required;
- Human hand-off: interaction was handed to humans to complete— could be a golden path or a failed one;
- User drop-out: the user dropped out.

These are some of the metrics you need to track:

- Prompt time-outs (NSP);
- Re-prompts: unrecognized;
- Failed to understand phrase—in-domain (should have understood) or out of domain;
- Failed to transcribe;
- Transcribed the wrong text from audio.

These navigation tracking points can provide useful info for conversational designers:

- Global shortcuts;
- Track end-of-speech detection times;
- Turn count, how many turns or responses in a conversation or skill;
- False positives;
- Correct reject;
- Confidence scores;
- Other matches with high confidence.

Key Takeaways

- Production design consists of conversational experience designers creating and fine-tuning flows based on high-level journey maps created by lead experience architects—analogous to a traditional experience designer skinning a wireframe.

- Users will likely see the conversational interface as the system, but it's just the access point, and success hinges on whether the IDW understands language and context deeply enough to determine the intention.

- Evolving the experiences users have with an IDW requires tools that let you analyze and report on interactions between users and IDWs in real time.

- Hyperautomation involves making sense of massive amounts of information that includes what users bring to the table (both how they communicate their needs and whatever supporting documents and data they provide), internal data stores, and information coming in from connected devices involved in any given experience.

- Following best practices for analyzing and reporting will allow you to iterate new solutions faster and accomplish far more.

Visit Invisiblemachines.ai for more information on production design efforts in hyperautomation.

CHAPTER 17

Best Practices in Conversational Design

As an interface, conversation can readily simulate human connection, making it easier to gather feedback. Imagine a conversational experience that helps new employees find the right classes to help them grow in their position. Instead of designing an interface that renders a browsable list of courses with general ratings, a conversational interface can ask a series of questions that disambiguate, contextualizing who the user is and what they might be interested in. Conversational AI can offer suggestions and get feedback on those suggestions, forging a process of discovery. As certain patterns are identified, users can be mapped to personas that help determine the class they should take. Through building thousands of conversational AI applications over the past decade, I've identified some best practices for conversational design. Here are 57 of the most valuable lessons I've learned. These aren't ranked in order of importance; instead, we'll start with the more general concepts and work toward the more specific ones.

1. **Remember that consistency is key:** Expectations don't stay flat, they increase or decrease. The safest bet is consistency across the experiences you offer. All of the goodwill and dazzle generated by an IDW that is super advanced in predicting and personalizing can be quickly squandered by another IDW that is dumb.

2. **Prioritize personalization over personality:** Creating a more personalized experience is more important than spending time giving the application a personality. Users will benefit more from an experience where their personal context is understood than one with an interesting IDW personality.

3. **Phrase prompts the right way:** Getting the right response depends on how you prompt a user. "Howdy" might mean "hello" to some and "how are you?" to others. "Hello" is more direct. Another example: "Can I ask you for your phone number?" Some people might provide a phone number, others might give a yes or no answer. More direct phrasing works better: "Can you please say your phone number one digit at a time?"

4. **Don't ask rhetorical questions:** Rhetorical questions can be confusing in conversations with humans, let alone conversations between IDWs and humans. Keep it simple and remember that your main objective is to help people.

5. **Use the question as part of the answer returned:** Add part of the question back into the answer you give so people know what the IDW interpreted from your interactions. For example: If a user asks the IDW what the weather is like, it returns, "The weather today is ..."

6. **Always put the question at the end:** People are used to transactional conversations that end in questions, so pose questions at the end of a statement to avoid interrupting a conversational workflow.

7. **Communicate conversationally:** Conversational applications (IDWs) should communicate conversationally. Avoid overly literate deliveries. We don't speak the same way that we write in articles, marketing materials, books, and so forth. A script that's too literate can ruin the tone of a conversational experience.

8. **Gauge for greetings:** Many users will greet a bot or IDW first. So even if your IDW starts the conversation with "Hello, how can I help you?" be prepared should the user reply with a simple "Hi."

9. **Note that more syllables help with speech recognition:** Short phrases can be more ambiguous and harder to recognize. Consider prompting for three-syllable responses.

10. **Different voices can signal different contexts:** Changing voices can be a helpful way to queue different contexts. You can adjust pitch in speech synthesis markup language (SSML) or choose different voice profiles. Something as simple as using a female voice for one task and male voice for another can help the user feel a transition.

11. **Don't overpromise:** Conversational designers should exercise caution to avoid overpromising. Even a general query such as "What can I help you with?" can be an overpromise if your IDW only knows three things. NLU engines are major culprits of failed attempts at using conversational AI because they can easily give the impression of sophisticated automation where none exists. NLU is important, but having it standing alone, disconnected from an ecosystem is about as useful as a customer support rep who can understand your problem but has no tools to help you with it. As an added layer, once you start creating experiences that are complex and intuitive, people will also have elevated expectations for future interactions. This is a part of the hype cycle—show users one trick, and they'll want something better next time—and the easiest way to avoid disappointment is by being clear and up-front about what your conversational AI is capable of.

12. **Orient users within the conversation:** When prompting for input, consider guiding their responses. For example, if they are looking for a location, it could be helpful to say, "There are four locations near you; you can ask me about any of them."

13. **On-boarding is ongoing and requires empathy:** Many users will be new to the experience of interacting with an IDW, and guiding them with empathetic cues can get them comfortably to speed.

    Here's a nice introduction from an IDW that provides a nice on-ramp to the kinds of experiences it can provide: "Hey, Teddy, I know you have a lot of meetings every week. Did you know I can help you schedule and reschedule them? Want to try now and see how it works?"

    A couple of days later, seeing that the user has taken advantage of its capabilities, the IDW can follow up and introduce some new complexity: "Hello again, Teddy! Glad I could help you get that meeting scheduled yesterday. Did you know that I operate over all of the communication channels your company uses? Try calling or texting me at this number. You can also ping me over Slack or email."

14. **Conversational markers let people know where they are:** Timelines, acknowledgments, and positive feedback help move the user through the conversation and set expectations. If an IDW is following up with a medical patient, for example, markers like these will help guide them through a set of questions:

    - "I will be asking you a few questions about your recovery."
    - "First, let me ask you . . ."
    - "Good job, and how many . . ."
    - "Got it; last question . . ."

15. **Visual cues are cool:** Where applicable, adding themed images that provide users with visual cues that their statements have been understood can provide a fun and fluid-feeling experience.

16. **Sometimes it's okay to guess what a user wants:** Especially with a simple Q&A, it's acceptable to guess what the user wants based on past experience. For example, if they ask, "What's the weather like?" assume they mean today and give them current conditions.

17. **Avoid making declarations about sensitive topics:** There are certain things that an IDW can be trained to detect about a user, such as age, country of origin, assigned gender, and even their current mood. But even if supporting data confirms the age of a user, the risk of offending the person by reminding them that they are 40 can be far greater than any perceived advantage. Similarly, if you're trying to show an IDW's chops at mood detection and fail, users will lose trust in the system. Saying "I can tell that you're upset. Rest assured, I'm here to help," is going to irritate someone who isn't actually upset. It's best to avoid using language that suggests the IDW has made these kinds of assessment. There are definite exceptions to this—specifically in health care settings—but unless there's a specific need to have an IDW acknowledge potentially sensitive topics, it's best practice to avoid it.

18. **Responses can be short:** When replying to users, it's best to keep your answers short. If the appropriate response is long, consider

asking clarifying questions and breaking the answer into a multi-turn exchange.

19. **Confirm transactions before completing them:** Always confirm with the user before completing a transaction, by asking for their approval. It can also be beneficial to follow up a transaction by restating what was completed and/or initiated (e.g., "Thank you for your purchase. Your order has been processed and you will receive a tracking number once your item has been shipped.").

20. **Promote your IDW's other features:** When appropriate, generally at the end of an interaction, consider letting the user know about other ways they can use your IDWs in the future. For example, at the end of a transaction, you might have your IDW say, "Thanks for your order. Feel free to text message me any time if you would like to know the status of your delivery or need to make a change to your order. "

21. **Be transparent with requests:** When asking users for information, be clear about why you need it. Healthy relationships are reciprocal, so take advantage of opportunities to explain what users get out of interactions (e.g., "Please type your email address so that I can keep you updated about your delivery.").

22. **Allow users to express confusion:** If a user doesn't reply to a question or command, consider prompting them that it's okay to say, "I don't know." Make sure they feel supported and know that it's fine in some cases to do nothing when prompted.

23. **Categorize responses:** You can create categories for happy, sad, serious, or funny responses to connect with the end user. When it comes to humor, people know that a machine's dialogue is written by humans. If it's appropriate, you can make an error message funny. It's a fine line though, so tread carefully.

24. **Negative responses:** Pay attention to negative indicators within responses ("not," "neither," "no," etc.). For example, when somebody is asking for a reminder call, they may say, "Not today." If your system is looking out for "not" rather than bypassing it, the outcome may be more desirable for the user.

25. **Responding to random questions:** For most IDWs, it is not necessary to field random questions such as "How are you?" Be a

machine, don't try to seem like a human. If it makes sense, then match the mood.

26. **Testing is critical:** Testing is critical, and HitL can help accelerate testing without compromising user experience. Here are a few helpful testing guidelines:

    - Set the stage for your test subjects (e.g., "You are trying to change your password and you are in a hurry.").
    - Test designs using HitL before building out automated versions to see if users actually appreciate the experience.
    - Have internal team members test out your experience.

27. **Survey your users:** You can use prompts such as these to get a sense of user satisfaction with the experience you're providing:

    - I will use the system in the future;
    - I would be happy to use the system again;
    - I think people will find this useful;
    - I think most people would not find this useful;
    - The system was easy to use;
    - The system understands what I say;
    - How could the system have been improved?
    - Did you like the system?

    You could also use a simple rating system to collect data (rate satisfaction/agreement from 1 to 5; gauge satisfaction level as dissatisfied, satisfied, loved it, etc.).

28. **Naming your IDWs:** Naming an IDW can be a powerful tool when appropriate. If your IDW has a proven track record of handling a whole array of customer requests, calling it Gary Guru can help give users the sense that they are in capable hands. As always, however, overpromising can be costly. A stagnant machine that can only perform a handful of tasks is not a Gary Guru.

29. **Design to have as few interactions as possible:** Imagine a user tells Domino's conversational application to "reorder." It might limit the number of potential interactions if the application responds, "I can reorder what you had last time: a large pizza with a large soda and Greek salad," rather than, "Which order would

you like to reorder, your order from March 7th, March 1st, or February 4th?"

30. **Design for interactive conversations:** It's useful to guess where the conversation will go and create your design around the expected interactive elements of a conversation.

> User: "What is the best eco-friendly cleaner?"
> IDW: "Dr. Bronner's makes the highest-rated eco-friendly cleaners."
> User: "Where can I get it?"

In this scenario, your IDW can anticipate that if someone is asking for a product recommendation, the next thing they will want to do is find out where to buy it.

31. **Consider adding weight to contextual data:** Adding weight to contextual data can help the user experience. For example, if your IDW is messaging you during the hours of 8 a.m.–5 p.m., it can assume you are working and put a higher weight on your context being at work (higher probability for that context).

32. **Context improves experience:** Keep your conversational application aware of the context: Is this visitor returning? Have they shopped here before? Did their package get delivered?

33. **Store context for future conversations:** Storing context will help you avoid the need to constantly disambiguate user questions. Once users know where they are, you can make assumptions for the near future.

34. **Disambiguate user requests:** After the user asks a question, it can be helpful to follow up with a clarifying question. For example, if the user asks, "Where is the nearest branch?" the IDW can respond, "Nearest branch to Denver or Boulder?"

35. **Show that the IDW understands:** Show that the IDW understands what is being said. Transcribing language visually is a great way to provide user confidence that the bot or IDW is understanding them. Similarly, you can design audio clues indicating comprehension in a voice-only setting.

36. **Flows that route to skills:** Design disambiguating flows that route to skills. Instead of trying to understand a specific request, you can train NLU to establish a general understanding. If a user

wants to do something involving passwords, you can create a flow that disambiguates and says, "Looks like you need help with logging in. I can do the following things . . ."

37. **Account for latency:** Latency refers to the lag experienced when retrieving data or connecting to third-party systems. Make sure you account for latency and provide cues to users (e.g., "Thank you for your patience while I'm connecting you."). Even a three-second dead spot can create an awkward experience. It's ideal to be fetching data ahead of time to avoid latency altogether, but if you can't, creating a way to keep the conversation going by avoiding silence will yield a better user experience.

38. **Use global commands:** Global commands are things users can employ to interrupt a conversational experience at any point in the interaction. They are most often used in interactive voice response (IVR) scenarios (e.g., allowing someone to cut in and say "agent" to get to a human operator). Always have global commands in place to make sure users don't get trapped in the conversation.

39. **Landmarking audio:** You can also use landmarking audio to communicate meaning for end users, for example, consistently using a specific sound that validates for a user that they've been understood. Something like how a car horn sound in newscast might prompt listeners that the traffic report is up next, consistently using appropriate sounds can build association between specific sounds and landmark moments in a conversation.

40. **Handling multiple intents:** There are several ways to account for multiple intents in conversational design. If the user states, "My order is the wrong size and color," consider asking which intent they would like to start with (size or color). Be prepared for problematic responses "both," or "neither." You can also start with one intent and cue the user. "Let's start with the sizing issue; was the garment too small or too large?"

41. **Regular use vs. one-time/periodic use:** Employees using a conversational interface are going to develop more familiarity with regular use, freeing designers up to use more efficient design paradigms. External users are far less likely to have or even develop the same level of familiarity with your conversational interface, which merits nonvisual skeuomorphic design. For contexts where both

one-time use and regular use are expected, designing for both is recommended.

42. **Time to resolution and perceived time to resolution:** Time to resolution (TTR) is the primary metric driving user satisfaction; however, perceived time to resolution (PTTR) is more important than actual time. There are ways to make users perceive TTR as shorter. Design considerations such as call backs rather than hold purgatory, eliminated unnatural pauses in conversation, and DTMF codes (enabling users to use numbers on the keypad to enter data during a phone experience) can all help decrease PTTR.

43. **Use confidence scores to train your IDW:** When building skills that use natural language understanding (NLU) engines, your IDW will return confidence scores for the intents (questions) that it collects from users. For example, if someone asks for help tracking their order and your IDW is not yet trained to handle this intent, it may return a low confidence score. In a scenario like this, you can add a low recognition response to get help from end users in training your engine.

    Best practices suggest that you are up-front and don't over-promise, saying something such as, "It seems like you are asking about tracking your order. I can get a human to help you with that."

44. **Generic confirmations are good for data collection:** Asking, "How are you feeling this morning?" or some other generic data confirmation can be good for both you and the person using the IDW. Remembering things puts a large cognitive burden on the user, and messaging is often used by people as an archival mechanism. Send them an SMS or email so they can retrieve the info in the future.

45. **Co-reference:** Co-referencing is used to keep track of subjects in a conversation, such as "he" or "she" referring to a person previously named in the conversation. For example:

    "Who founded your company?" "Where did he live?"

    "He" is a co-reference to the founder. You'll need to create a variable called "he," "she," or "they" and assign it a name so you can refer back to it if somebody types "he," "she," "they," or "their." Keeping track of co-references may require creating variable versions of each pronoun that adjust dynamically according to who you are referencing.

46. **Know when to allow barge-in:** As with human-to-human conversation, interactions between people and IDWs can be stifled by interruptions. Allowing users to barge in can be useful at times (being able to call out "operator" in the midst of a confusing interaction is a valuable lifeline) and troublesome at others (if a user interrupts an IDW as it's listing options with an unfamiliar response, confusion can ensue on both sides).

    It's always helpful to let users know that, although they might be waiting for a prompt, the process is still moving forward. Over a video channel you could mitigate this by creating video loops to indicate a productive pause.

    During informational prompts, listing options before asking the user what they want to do can deter them from barging in early.

47. **Speech recognition accuracy trumps price and latency:** A less-expensive solution that can't accurately interpret user requests isn't going to be worth any amount of money saved. A system that is swift but inaccurate is ultimately faster at not being good.

48. **Consider hybrid solutions when using text-to-speech:** You can have a human record conversational prompts and then use text-to-speech (TTS) with Speech Synthesis Markup Language (SSML) to fill in the gaps. For instance, if you record a member of your HR team reading a list of options but don't have a follow-up cue in that person's voice saying, "I'm not sure I heard you; can you repeat that?" you can create that script with TTS and tweak the voice to sound like its human counterpart. This method may not be perfect, but it can still serve the user well.

49. **Consider voice ID for authenticating users:** In situations that require sensitive data, authenticating your users voice can be a helpful part of the experience

50. **Answering questions from a third party:** Instead of loading FAQs or search results in NLU models to provide the answers first party, consider scenarios where the IDW should answer with third-party results. The IDW can say, "I don't know the answer, but I found this by doing a web search." In essence, handle it like

a person would. By presenting the user with third-party info, you can allow them to disambiguate the information.

51. **Use voice channels where appropriate:** Voice-enabling a website just for the sake of doing it has limited value, but using the web and voice together to create multimodal interactions can be very powerful. Just like in real conversation, there will always be instances where it's more efficient to show someone a video clip or visual aid than it is to try and explain it via text or speech.

52. **Dynamic grammars should be built in:** Always consider dynamic grammars for things like alphanumeric responses, names, or email addresses. For instance, if someone types the name of a colleague and spells it wrong, the system can apply fuzzy-match to determine that they meant "Josh," even though they typed "Joshh." Similarly, if they typed "josh@gmale.com," it could assume that they probably meant gmail.com.

53. **Handling errors in conversation design:** Set expectations by responding with something such as, "Sorry, I am not trained in that area yet" or "I didn't understand your question." If the IDW does not receive a response over voice channels, respond by prompting the user to repeat themselves by saying something such as, "Hmm, I didn't hear that. Can you repeat yourself?" You can also use alternatives like DTMF (dual tone multi-frequency—dialing numbers to get menu options), or offer instructions such as, "Please say 'yes' or 'no.'"

    If the intent was recognized but an error occurred, let the user know by saying, "I encountered an error while . . ." If the intent was misunderstood by the NLU engine and your IDW discovers it, offer other options. It's possible there was a misunderstanding and/or the user changed their mind and simply wants to do something else. Funny or cute error responses are great, but be careful—if you do it too often, it becomes annoying, like telling the same joke over and over.

54. **Don't build one-size-fits-all IDWs:** One-size-fits-all is often one-size-fits-none. Don't dumb your IDWs down to the lowest common denominator by trying to make them all do everything across multiple channels. Build a state-of-the-art IDW for each channel.

Utilize the features in each channel to their fullest, and write dialogue appropriately for the given context. In an ecosystem that's built for hyperautomation, individual state-of-the-art IDWs can be sequenced to engage in workflows together, creating better-than-human experiences for users. In a similar vein, not all IDWs need to be personal assistants. Some machines or IDWs work optimally on a specific set of tasks.

55. **Build in pairs:** If you're designing conversational experiences all by yourself, you're likely to miss things, On the other hand, building with a group of 10, progress can stall as everyone struggles to get on the same page. Working in pairs can be ideal, if only for the simple fact that the most meaningful conversations tend to occur between two people. On a more practical level, when two people are working in tandem on conversational design (as opposed to handing the project back and forth) you can have one person focus on the logical, systems-thinking side of things while the other homes in on design elements. This way, fewer things fall through the cracks, and designs are tested and improved upon more efficiently.

56. **Consider the ongoing evolution of conversation with machines:** Conversations with computers will evolve, potentially creating a new language, more efficient than formal English. We see this already with text messaging shorthand like "BRB"—a language dubbed "textese." Something similar will emerge as people find shorthand ways of communicating with conversational technologies. This begins with routine users finding the most direct ways to communicate needs to the IDWs in their ecosystem. It evolves as analysts notice trends in the ways users are communicating conversationally and experience designers encourage users to utilize these new ways of communicating.

57. **Keeping IDWs outside the social circle has benefits:** IDWs can be anthropomorphic to great effect, ranging from giving friendly reminders to communicating with urgency when we ignore a prompt for immediate action. With typical human interactions, when someone is friendly or brash, we're inclined to respond in ways that correlate to social ranking. These kinds of intuitive responses can take many forms. Someone being friendly as they

prompt you to take action might put you at ease because they are being helpful, but it might also signal an alarm if you perceive their friendliness as an attempt to climb past you in a social hierarchy. Similarly, if someone is being aggressive or forceful in their reminders, it might be felt as an attempt to show dominance. IDWs, on the other hand, can remind us relentlessly without it feeling like a threat. As machines that we are not in direct competition with and that don't have ulterior motives, IDWs sit outside of our social circles. That being said, how you choose to anthropomorphize your IDWs can also have sizeable consequences in terms of how users react to them (make them seem too human, and you could risk bringing them inside the social circle). It's all about balance, which makes anthropomorphism—along with skeuomorphism—something that should be given careful consideration.

As the volume of information here suggests, production design in the realm of hyperautomation requires a great deal of strategy and flexibility. By keeping these best practices in mind, however, you can mitigate some of the discomfort and make faster progress.

Two Important Morphisms

When designing experiences that employ conversational AI, it's tempting to want to create something as natural-feeling as possible—but when designing for productivity, that's often the wrong move. Natural pauses and witticisms meant to make an IDW seem more relatable can easily go too far and distract from the task at hand. While these kinds of touches are useful in entertainment products, they should be used sparingly in productivity tools. This is why *skeuomorphism* and *anthropomorphism* both play important roles in conversational AI design, sometimes working in complementary ways.

In visual design, *skeuomorphism* is the concept of making digital things look like their real-world counterparts (see Figure 17.1). When users encountered the calculator in early versions of Mac OS, the shaded buttons made it look similar to the calculator in their desk drawer. As user adoption widens, the need for those kinds of visual cues dissipates. We've reached the nonvisual skeuomorphic phase of evolution with

SKEUOMORPHIC DESIGN   **EFFICIENT DESIGN PARADIGMS**

98658 / 1256 * 1984   98658 / 1256 * 1984

Intelligent
Digital Worker

FIGURE 17.1   *Skeuomorphic design as it relates to conversational
design. (OneReach.ai)*

conversational design. This means we're following the same track as
visual design in terms of users understanding the technology. To a conversational designer, this might mean adding a few interactions to make
sure users understand the nature of the experience they're engaged in,
such as pausing early in the conversation to remind them that they are
communicating with an IDW built to handle specific requests.

Visual designers employ anthropomorphism by imbuing objects with human traits and characteristics in order to make them more relatable. When used in conversational design, anthropomorphism creates the feeling or perception of a human-to-human relationship between the IDW and the user. If used successfully, this lever can foster a sense of connection, trust, and loyalty. But this powerful tool must be used conscientiously; we don't want to fool an end-user's senses into believing they are interacting with a person they can have a meaningful relationship with. If a user comes to trust an IDW the way they might trust a friend or colleague, they are at risk of having that trust compromised—by being roped into a sales pitch, for example—which could have long-lasting negative consequences. Use care in making the IDW more relatable and the interaction more authentic without crossing over into deceit.

It's also important to keep your sights on the objective of your design. In productivity apps, where the goal is to get users from A to B as quickly and efficiently as possible, features meant to make the IDW seem more human can quickly become tiresome—analogous to a waiter hell-bent on light conversation when you're in a rush to order.

In gaming apps, users spend hours getting immersed in drawn-out storylines with characters that simulate human behavior. Users aren't looking for reduced friction and probably expect to become frustrated; in fact, a user throwing a controller across the room after the 20th fail represents a big win for that game's designer. But productivity calls for as little friction—and human simulation—as possible. You don't need extra explanations, personality traits, or yuks to help get the job done. Sometimes it's best to just let a machine be a machine.

The intention of both skeuomorphic and anthropomorphic design is to help users to engage with your objective—in essence offering them a shorter on-ramp by adding familiarity and relatability via nuance and timing. This process takes more effort, and getting it right requires a high level of sophistication. But once the technology is widespread enough to already be familiar—at a point where users don't need as many visual cues—the design load is lighter.

Note that the relationship between these morphisms can become entangled. Anthropomorphism taken too far becomes a simulation of humans—and then a skeuomorphism of humans. This gets weird fast, taking conversational experiences into an uncanny valley of creepy

3D avatars and too-human rubber-faced robots—which can create in users a sense of unease or even disgust. The lesson here is that these powerful design tools should be applied with a light touch.

Key Takeaway: Production Design Checklist

To follow is a cheat sheet of points to consider when designing conversational experiences.

Findable

Strive to design experiences that make it easy for users to find what they are looking for. It's also important that the information provided is concise—that users are not overloaded with extraneous data.

- Can users quickly and easily locate what they are seeking?
- How is findability accounted for across channels, devices, and time?
- Are there multiple ways to access things?
- How do external and internal search engines show information?
- Is information formatted with results in mind?
- How are the delivered results made useful?
- Are multiple ways to reach content supported?
- Is search easy to find and consistently placed? Is search easy to use? Does it support revision and refinement?
- Are query builders used effectively? (Spell-checking, stemming, concept searching, and thesaural searching.)
- Are useful results available at the top of the in-site results list?
- Did we strive to design navigable websites and locatable objects so users can find what they need?
- Did we strive to ensure users aren't overloaded with extraneous information?

PRODUCTION DESIGN CHECKLIST

A cheat sheet for considerations when designing conversational experiences

FINDABLE

- Can users quickly and easily locate what they are seeking?
- How is findability accounted for across channels, devices, and time?
- Are there multiple ways to access things?
- How do external and internal search engines show information?
- Is information formatted with results in mind?
- How are the delivered results made useful?
- Are multiple ways to reach content supportive?
- Is search easy to find and consistently placed? Is search easy to support revision and refinement?
- Are query builders used effectively? (spell-checkup, stemming, concept searching, and thesaural searching)
- Are useful results available at the top of the in-site results list?
- Did we strive to design navigable web sites and locatable objects, so users can find what they need?
- Were we conscious so that users aren't overloaded with extraneous information?

ACCESSIBLE

- Does the experience span across channels, devices, and time?
- How consistent is the experience across channels that have not been previously used?
- Does it meet the levels of accessibility compliance to account for users with disabilities?
- Have you accounted for the fact that upwards of 20% or more of the world's population has a disability?
- Does the system should speak the users' language, with words, phrases and concepts familiar to the user, rather than system-oriented terms?
- Does it follow real-world conventions, making information appear in a natural and logical order?
- Is it possible to move through the site without experiencing click fatigue?
- Is there enough resilience for a pervasive information architecture model to shape and adapt itself to specific users, needs and seeking strategies?
- Is there enough consistency for a pervasive IA model to suit the purpose, the contexts, and the people it is designed for and to maintain the same logic along different media, environments and times in which it acts?

CLEAR

- Is it easy to understand?
- Is the target demographics' reading level and writing tone needed?
- Is the path to task completion simple and free of distraction?
- Would a user find it easy to describe the user experience?
- Are you employing aesthetic and minimalist design so that dialogues don't contain information which is irrelevant or rarely needed?
- Do extra units of information in a dialogue compete with the relevant units of information, thus diminishing their relative?
- Is it clear what's being searched for, what the query is and how many results are returned?
- Are labels clear and meaningful?
- Is the information content conveyed such that it can be grasped quickly and accurately?
- Is the disclosed information discriminable, or able to be distinguished accurately?
- Is the information legible and easy to read?
- Is there consistency to your unique design, so that it conforms with user expectations?
- Are there reduction measures in place so that a pervasive IA model can manage large information sets and minimize stress and frustration associated with choosing from an ever growing set of information sources, services, and goods?

COMMUNICATIVE

- Are the status, location and permissions of the under obvious and accounted for?
- How is messaging used through out? Is it effective for the tasks and is it supportive of the context?
- Does the navigation and messaging help establish a sense of place that is consistent across channels, contexts and tasks?
- Is the system status visible so that users are always informed about what's going on, through appropriate feedback within reasonable time?
- Are you minimizing the user's memory load by making objects, actions, and options visible? The user should not have to remember information from one part of the dialogue to another. Instructions for use of the system should be visible or easily retrievable whenever appropriate.
- Does it orient the user to what this site is about and content is available?
- Is it clear where the user is, both in relation to the site and where they are in the site?
- Is the dialogue is self-descriptive so that each step is immediately comprehensible through feedback from the system and is explained to the user on request?
- Is the user's attention is directed towards information required, making it easy to detect?

USEFUL

- Is it usable? Are users' needs solved without massive frustration or abandon?
- Does it serve new and returning users in ways that satisfy their needs uniquely?
- Are there navigation options that lead where users may want to go next? Are they clearly labeled?
- Help users recognize, diagnose, and recover from errors. Errors should be expressed in plain language precisely indicate the problem, and constructively suggest a solution.
- Does it serve users who have been there before and know what they're looking for?
- Does it highlight the best ways to reach content? In search: Are useful components displayed per set? Are the results grouped in a useful way?
- Is there a free navigation options that lead me where I'd want to go next?
- Are they clearly labeled?
- With ease of use remaining vital, the interface-centered methods and perspectives of human-computer interaction do not address all dimensions of web design, are you going beyond basic usability?
- We must have the courage and creativity to ask whether our products and systems are useful, and to apply our knowledge of craft and medium to define innovative solutions that are more useful. As a practitioner, you are fighting the urge to remain content with painting inside the lines drawn by managers?
- Is the dialogue is suitable for a task—does it supports the user in the effective and efficient completion of the task?
- Is there enough correlation so that there's the capability of a pervasive information architecture model to suggest relevant connections among pieces of information, services, and goods to help users achieve explicit goals or stimulate latent needs?

Originally sourced and diagrammed by Abby Covert and the Understanding Group

FIGURE 17.2   *Key design patterns to sequence for conversation design.*

PRODUCTION DESIGN CHECKLIST

A cheat sheet for considerations when designing conversational experiences

CREDIBLE

- Is the design fitting to the context and the audience?
- Is your content recent and updated often?
- Is promotional content used sparingly?

- Is it easy to contact a person?
- Is it easy to verify credentials?
- Do you have help/support content where it is needed?

- Does the user feel like their privacy and security is top priority? This is especially important when asking for sensitive private data.
- Even though it is better if the system can be used without documentation, can you provide

- help and documentation in a way that's easy to search, focused on the user's task, lists concrete steps to be carried out, and isn't too large?
- Do the design elements that influence whether users trust and believe what we tell them adhere to guidelines proposed by the Web Credibility Project?.

CONTROLLABLE

- Is any information a user may need easily available?
- Will the user be able to accomplish reasonable tasks related to the experience?
- When errors do occur, how quickly can they be resolved?

- How well are errors anticipated and eliminated? Do you have a Human-in-the-Loop (as a solution for unforeseen errors?
- Are features offered that allow the user to tailor information or functionality to their need?
- Are ends and other important controls clearly marked?

- Are you making is easy for users to system functions by mistake—Is there a clearly marked "emergency exit" to leave the unwanted state without having to go through an extended dialogue?
- Have you been careful to design so errors are prevented from occurring by either eliminating error-prone

- conditions or checking for them and presenting users with a confirmation option before they commit to the action?
- Accelerators—unseen by the novice user—may often speed up the interaction for the expert user such that the system can cater to both inexperienced and experienced users. Do you allow users to tailor frequent actions for flexibility and efficiency of use?

- Is the dialogue is controllable when the user is able to initiate and control the direction and pace of the interaction until the point at which the goal has been met?
- Is the dialogue is error tolerant if, despite evident errors in input, the intended result may be achieved with either no or minimal action by the user?
- Is the dialogue is capable of individualization when the interface software can be modified to suit user needs?

VALUABLE

- Is the experience desirable to the user?
- Does it maintain consistent expectations throughout the interaction across channels, without overpromising?
- Can a user easily describe the value?

- How is success measured? Does it contribute to the bottom line?
- Does it improve customer satisfaction?
- Are breadth and depth balanced?

- Has your quest for efficiency been tempered by an appreciation for the power and value of image, identity, brand, and other elements of emotional design?
- In an effort to deliver value to sponsors, non-profits need the

- user experience to advance their mission. With for-profits, it must contribute to the bottom line and improve customer satisfaction.
- Are you presenting the value of UX?

LEARNABLE

- Can it be grasped quickly?
- What is offered to make complicated processes more simple?
- Is it memorable for the right reasons?

- Is it easy to see steps taken to resolve issues?
- Does it behave consistently enough to be predictable?
- Users should not have to wonder whether different words, situations, or actions mean the same thing. Are you following platform conventions for consistency and standards.

- A dialog supports suitability for learning, if it guides the user through the learning time.
- Is the meaning clearly understandable, unambiguous, interpretable, and recognizable?

DELIGHTFUL

- What differentiates it from other similar experiences or competitors?
- What omni-channel ties can be explored that delight?
- How are expectations not just met but exceeded?
- What are you providing that is expected?

- What ordinary pieces can be made extraordinary?
- Historically, "delight" has not been talked about in regards to heuristic measurement, yet consideration of differentiators and goals around exceeding user expectations are becoming increasingly important to consumers—especially as we explore cross channel solutions.

Originally sourced and diagrammed by Abby Covet and the Understanding Group

FIGURE 17.3 *Key design patterns to sequence for conversation design.*

Scan to get the updated check list and related content.

Accessible

Accessibility is a crucial component of all good design. Keep it at the core of your strategy to make sure everyone has access to technology and to identify opportunities for personalized service design.

- Does the experience span across channels, devices, and time?
- How consistent is the experience across channels that have not been previously used?
- Does it meet the levels of accessibility compliance to account for users with disabilities?
- Have you accounted for the fact that about 15% of the world's population has a disability? Just as our buildings have elevators and ramps, our websites need to be accessible to everyone.
- Is there a good match between system and the real world? The system should speak the users' language, with words, phrases, and concepts familiar to the user, rather than system-oriented terms. Follow real-world conventions, making information appear in a natural and logical order.
- Is it possible to move through the experience without experiencing click fatigue?
- Is there enough resilience for a pervasive information architecture model to shape and adapt itself to specific users, needs, and seeking strategies?
- Is there enough consistency for a pervasive information architecture model to suit the purposes, the contexts, and the people it is designed for and to maintain the same logic along different media, environments, and times in which it acts?

Clear

Great conversational designs begin with clarity of purpose. It should be easy for every user to understand their options and make informed decisions about how to proceed through their journey.

- Is it easy to understand?
- Is the target demographics' reading language being considered?
- Is the path to task completion simple and free of distraction?
- Would a user find it easy to describe the user experience?
- Are you employing aesthetic and minimalist design so that dialogues don't contain information that is irrelevant or rarely needed?
- Do extra units of information in a dialogue compete with the relevant units of information, thus diminishing their relative relevance?
- Is it clear what's being searched for, what the query is, and how many results are returned?
- Are labels clear and meaningful?
- Is the information content conveyed such that it can be grasped quickly and accurately?
- Is the displayed information discriminable or able to be distinguished accurately?
- Is the information legible and easy to read?
- Is there consistency to your unique design, so that it conforms with user expectations?
- Are there reduction measures in place so that a pervasive information architecture model can manage large information sets and minimize stress and frustration associated with choosing from an ever growing set of information sources, services, and goods?

Communicative

Conversational interfaces should communicate relevant information in ways that are helpful and easy to follow. Take care to keep users well oriented throughout their journey. Remember that these experiences are multi-channel and can share information across many different modalities.

- How is messaging used throughout? Is it effective for the tasks, and is it supportive of the context?
- Are status, location, and permissions obvious and accounted for?
- Does the navigation and messaging help establish a sense of place that is consistent across channels, contexts, and tasks?
- Is the system status visible so that users are always informed about what is going on, through appropriate feedback within reasonable time?
- Are you minimizing the user's memory load by making objects, actions, and options visible? (The user should not have to remember information from one part of the dialogue to another. Instructions for use of the system should be visible or easily retrievable whenever appropriate.)
- Does it orient the user to what the experience, site, application, etc. is about and options that are available?
- Is it clear where the user is, both in terms of which experience and where they are in the experience?
- Is the dialogue self-descriptive so that each step is immediately comprehensible through feedback from the system or is it explained to the user on request?
- Is the user's attention is directed toward information required, making it easy to detect?
- Is there enough of a pervasive information architecture model to help users reduce disorientation, build a sense of place, and increase legibility and way-finding across digital, physical, and cross-channel environments?

Useful

If your design isn't useful, it has no purpose. The goal should be to create meaningful experiences that solve problems in clear and direct ways. Users should feel empowered by the design decisions you're making.

- Is it usable? Are users' needs solved without massive frustration or abandon?
- Does it serve new and returning users in ways that satisfy their needs uniquely?

- Are there navigation options that lead where users may want to go next? Are they clearly labeled?
- It's important to help users recognize, diagnose, and recover from errors. Are the errors expressed in plain language that precisely indicates the problem—and constructively suggests a solution?
- Does it serve users who have been here before and know what they're looking for?
- Does it highlight the best ways to reach content? In search: Are useful components displayed per result? Are the results grouped in a useful way?
- Are there a few navigation options that lead me where I'd want to go next?
- Are they clearly labeled?
- With ease of use remaining vital, the interface-centered methods and perspectives of human-computer interaction do not address all dimensions. Are you going beyond basic usability?
- We must have the courage and creativity to ask whether our products and systems are useful and to apply our deep knowledge of craft and medium to define innovative solutions that are more useful. As a practitioner, are you fighting the urge to remain content with painting inside the lines drawn by managers?
- Is the dialogue suitable for a task? Does it supports the user in the effective and efficient completion of the task?
- Is there enough correlation so that there's the capability of a pervasive information architecture model to suggest relevant connections among pieces of information, services, and goods to help users achieve explicit goals or stimulate latent needs?

Credible

Credibility is key when working with conversational AI. Establishing credibility can be as simple as making it easy for users to locate your credentials and as nuanced as designing personalized experiences that meet users at their needs.

- Is the design fitting to the context and the audience?
- Is your content recent and updated often?

- Is promotional content used sparingly?
- Is it easy to contact a person?
- Is it easy to verify credentials?
- Do you have help/support content where it is needed?
- Does the user feel like their privacy and security is top priority? This is especially important when asking for sensitive private data.
- Even though it is better if the system can be used without documentation, can you provide help and documentation in a way that's easy to search, focused on the user's task, lists concrete steps to be carried out, and isn't too large?
- Do the design elements that influence whether users trust and believe what we tell them adhere to guidelines proposed by the Web Credibility Project?

Controllable

Give users control over their journey by offering relevant features and making it easy for them to backtrack. Depending on the nature of the experience you can also offer varying degrees of customization. On the back end, make it easy for a human-in-the-loop to jump into a conversation and steer its course.

- Is any information a user may need easily available?
- Will the user be able to accomplish reasonable tasks related to the experience?
- How well are errors anticipated and eliminated? Do you have a human-in-the-loop as a solution for unforeseen errors?
- When errors do occur, how quickly can they be resolved?
- Are features offered that allow the user to tailor information or functionality to their need?
- Are exits and other important controls clearly marked?
- Are you making is easy for users to backtrack when they initiate system functions by mistake—is there a clearly marked "emergency exit" to leave the unwanted state without having to go through an extended dialogue?
- Have you been careful to design so errors are prevented from occurring by either eliminating error-prone conditions or checking for

them and presenting users with a confirmation option before they commit to the action?

- Accelerators—unseen by the novice user—may often speed up the interaction for the expert user such that the system can cater to both inexperienced and experienced users. Do you allow users to tailor frequent actions for flexibility and efficiency of use?
- Is the dialogue controllable when the user is able to initiate and control the direction and pace of the interaction until the point at which the goal has been met?
- Is the dialogue error tolerant? May the intended result be achieved, despite evident errors in input, with either no or minimal action by the user?
- Is the dialogue capable of individualization when the interface software can be modified to suit user needs?

Valuable

If users feel like there is value in an experience, they'll return to it again and again. Value is a cumulative expression of the design thinking that goes into every element of the experience.

- Is the experience desirable to the user?
- Does it maintain consistent expectations throughout the interaction across channels, without overpromising?
- Can a user easily describe the value?
- How is success measured? Does it contribute to the bottom line?
- Does it improve customer satisfaction?
- Are breadth and depth balanced?
- Has your quest for efficiency been tempered by an appreciation for the power and value of image, identity, brand, and other elements of emotional design?
- In an effort to deliver value to sponsors, nonprofits need the user experience to advance their mission. With for-profits, it must contribute to the bottom line and improve customer satisfaction. Are you presenting the value of UX?

Learnable

Conversational interfaces should be easy for users to understand and acclimate to using. They exist, in part, to simplify complex processes—something they should do with consistency and clarity.

- Can it be grasped quickly?
- What is offered to make complicated processes more simple?
- Is it memorable for the right reasons?
- Is it easy to see steps taken to resolve issues?
- Does it behave consistently enough to be predictable?
- Users should not have to wonder whether different words, situations, or actions mean the same thing. Are you following platform conventions for consistency and standards?
- A dialog supports suitability for learning if it guides the user through the learning stages minimizing the learning time. Do your dialogues support suitability for learning?
- Is the meaning clearly understandable, unambiguous, interpretable, and recognizable?

Delightful

Historically, "delight" has not been talked about in regard to heuristic measurement, yet consideration of differentiators and goals around exceeding user expectations are becoming increasingly important to consumers—especially as you explore cross-channel solutions.

- What differentiates it from other similar experiences or competitors?
- What omni-channel ties can be explored that delight?
- How are expectations not just met but exceeded?
- What are you providing that is expected?
- What ordinary pieces can be made extraordinary?

Visit invisiblemachines.ai for updated information on best practices in conversational design.

PART IV

Conclusion

CHAPTER 18

Where Do We Go from Here?

I worked as a sound editor for Warner Bros. in the 1990s, during the seismic shift that carried the film industry from analog to digital. As celluloid became a thing of the past, I realized that some of the most talented and experienced people I worked alongside on films—like *Prince of Tides*, *Deep Impact*, *Thin Red Line*, and *Galaxy Quest*—were at risk of losing their jobs to those with the chief qualification of knowing how to use technology better. This posed a serious problem.

While I was fortunate in that I understood how to use computers, I also recognized that, while digital technology certainly made it easier to edit films, it didn't make it any easier to edit films well. The best sound and video editors I knew had spent their entire professional lives learning the distinct rhythms of filmic storytelling. Their hands-on experience cutting ribbons made them the ideal people to develop digital editing techniques. To pass the craft of editing over to those who were simply better at using computers would have meant losing generations of experience and nuance. I made it my mission to ensure that didn't happen. What I came to realize is that analog editors were most comfortable using an interface that mimicked the tactile tools they'd been using their whole lives. There was a decision-making pattern inherent to those tools that was beneficial to anyone using digital tools—whether they were veterans or new to the process.

This work forged a passion that followed as I left the film industry behind and later founded an agency focused on experience design. My goal was never to design the most beautiful button or disruptive app—it was to make sure that, as technology raced ahead, people weren't getting left behind. Making it easier for people to create and use technology effectively meant more people were able to benefit from it. As technology continues to augment and manage key parts of our daily lives (everything from international infrastructures to personal calendars), it's important that everyone has opportunities to engage and create with it.

Exponential leaps forward in technology happen almost every day, and they continually threaten to widen the gap between humans and machines. By enabling the mass adoption of conversational AI and hyperautomation through simplified design and deployment, we can use these powerful emergent technologies to elevate those who can benefit most from using it. As I see it, the ultimate goal of hyperautomation is turning anyone with a problem to solve into a software designer. I've been developing ways to wrangle these technologies for decades now, and the methods and ecosystems described in this book represent the best ideas I've come up with for bringing hyperautomation to life in ways that can benefit all of humanity.

To reference a movie I didn't work on, *Her* handled the breadth and nuance of conversational AI beautifully. The relationship between the film's protagonist, Theodore, and his artificially intelligent virtual assistant, Samantha, touches on many of the concepts we've explored in these pages. Samantha isn't an app like Siri and Alexa, it's an operating system. Samantha is Theodore's gateway to all the different technologies he encounters (essentially turning apps into skills). Theodore is sitting at a desktop computer when he installs this new OS, but once he's accustomed to interacting with Samantha, he can leverage technology conversationally just about anywhere he goes. Samantha sees what Theodore sees via the camera on the phone he carries in his shirt pocket. He speaks to her using an earpiece, and when she wants to show him something, she sends an image to any nearby device. Through Samantha, technology has become an extension of Theodore, giving him new capabilities.

Along with the other tangible and artificial characters in the film, the relationship between human and machine careens into new corners of psychology and theoretical models for superintelligence that could easily fill two more books. Regardless, if you imagine everyone having Theodore's relationship with technology, the possibilities to do amazing things mushroom quickly. This is how technology can continue to grow and evolve without leaving people behind.

Twenty years ago, I embarked on a career in experience design with that question in mind: How can we grow technology while making it accessible? Clearly we would never be able to slow it down so that people could catch up. I challenged my fellow experience design practitioners to take up the cause and built up *UX Magazine* with the goal of creating a vibrant community where we could share our successes and failures and improve our craft together.

The conversational AI platform I created that was referenced throughout this book is another extension of that same mission. By giving anyone access to an open system for orchestrating their ecosystem of technologies through a conversational interface, the process of software creation becomes democratized. Anyone among us can devise, contribute to, execute, and evolve better-than-human solutions to high-level problems.

To borrow an overused quote from another movie I didn't work on, *Spider-Man* (2002), "With great power comes great responsibility." The power of hyperautomation is gargantuan, and wielding it properly requires responsibility and vision. We're alive during a curious impasse in human history, when our ingenuity will be required to outrun the destruction wrought by our impulses. So while it's important that we all have a say in how technology enables our progress, it's equally important that we don't let the wrong forces dictate it.

As I noted in the beginning of this book, the status quo is a death sentence. This certainly holds true for businesses moving into the immediate future, but it also applies to the human race. The global pandemic and escalating climate change have made it clear that the current ways of doing things are utterly unsustainable. If we stay this broken course, our species seems destined for extinction. Technology has the power to alter our course and perhaps provide a pathway to sustainability.

Another point to consider ties into the modular nature of the various technologies that we can orchestrate within an ecosystem built for hyperautomation. The only way I can see these ecosystems thriving is if they are open. In an open ecosystem made up of modular technologies, those individual technologies immediately become commodified. If I have a truly open system and improved NLU/NLP technology becomes available, it doesn't really matter to me who the vendor is: If it's truly better tech, I'll want to use it and I'll be able to.

Suppose my organization uses most of Salesforce's tools within our ecosystem. If we discover a better tool for a specific functionality elsewhere and begin using it, it won't take Salesforce long to realize that there's a better piece of tech competing for their market share. Salesforce will be motivated to improve on that functionality and win back customers. Following today's common business practices, they might even want to acquire whatever company is making the better tool. But what if the tool was created by people working in the decentralized autonomous organizations we described earlier in this book? A DAO is essentially a group of people working together on projects they agree they want to take on at rates they set themselves operating from a shared pool of resources, all of it nested securely in the blockchain. The whole point of these organizations is autonomy, so why would they want to become part of a restrictive business model where their efforts benefit those at the top instead of their own team?

This creates a paradoxical situation for traditional organizations, one that begins to question their very relevance as entities. I described a scenario earlier in which modular pieces of photo editing software accessed by conversational interface would make Photoshop's graphical UI rather meaningless. If I ask my device to help me crop a photo, I just want quick access to the best cropping tool available, I don't care if it's part of Photoshop's suite of tools. An open ecosystem orchestrating modular technologies has no real use for licensed bundles of technology. In order to continually evolve and improve, open ecosystems will value flexibility over all else. By extension, in a world that is driven by hyperautomation, why would Adobe or Salesforce want to be in the business of creating technologies that live in closed systems? At a certain point, the question becomes, why have a centralized organization at all? When the traditional organizational structure becomes obsolete in this way, the utter insanity of having a handful of people at the top acquiring massively disproportionate amounts of wealth at the expense of the hundreds and thousands underneath them will be impossible to ignore.

I know, pump the brakes, right? If this is the future that awaits us, why should you feel compelled to upend your entire company in order to undertake the colossal task of hyperautomation? Sure, it sounds very alluring to have an organization continually improving its ability to be self-driving, but why bother having an organization at all? My answer to this question is that we begin the journey toward hyper-automation inside the organizations that we have right now. We should do our best to benefit the people working within our organizations as well as those who use our services. We need a world of competent, ethical open systems running hyperautomation. What we do now within our existing organizations will likely lead to an endgame that renders those very organizations irrelevant, but what we're ultimately talking about building is a structure within which technology can benefit all of humankind equally.

This is a frantically fraught moment in history: the pandemic is still flaring, climate change is accelerating, and a war is unfolding in Europe. Hopefully it's obvious that we need powerful problem-solving tools to help us fix massive problems intelligently, not for the benefit of business but for the benefit of humankind. On a very basic level, we can also use technology to create experiences that make people feel good. We can forge an economy where we're valued by how good we make other people feel. Reducing these activities to a chemical compound might seem a bit cynical, but an economy based on dopamine fits right in with the idea of scoring social interactions on the blockchain. Life could be a lot less stressful if the economy we interact with every day is centered on experiences that produce happiness.

Things may seem bleak right now, but we're actually at a truly momentous moment in our history as a species. The situation is dire, but we have everything we need to save ourselves. To quote a couple movies I did work on, "Life will go on, we will prevail" (*Deep Impact*, 1998) "Never give up! Never surrender!" (*Galaxy Quest*, 1999).

My team has played a part in designing AI solutions that have helped people quit smoking and contributed to curbing sex traffick-ing. I've seen firsthand how powerful technology can be in terms of changing individual behaviors and disrupting criminal actions. Hyper-automation might very well represent our best chance at getting out of the massive pickle our industrialized world has dunked itself in. For that to happen, however, it needs to be implemented in an inclusive manner that enables all of us.

My hope is that this book has opened your mind to the possibilities and challenges presented by hyperautomation. It's taken me 20 years to articulate my vision for how we can put these powerful technologies to work for us, but it will only take a sliver of that time for hyper-automation to reshape our world. Together, we can make sure those sweeping changes carry us forward into a brighter future.

Visit invisiblemachines.ai for more of Robb's insights into the rapidly evolving world of hyperautomation.

Notes

Preface

1. "Why 'Total Experience (TX)' is Gartner's top technology trend for 2022," Clover Infotech, December 22, 2021, https://www.cloverinfotech.com/blog/why-total-experience-tx-is-gartners-top-technology-trend-for-2022/.

Chapter 1

1. Jack Loechner, "90% of Today's Data Created in Two Years," Media-Post, quoting IBM Marketing Cloud, "10 Key Marketing Trends for 2017," December 22, 2016, https://www.mediapost.com/publications/article/291358/90-of-todays-data-created-in-two-years.html.
2. Will Knight, "Meet the Chinese Finance Giant That's Secretly an AI Company," *MIT Technology Review*, June 16, 2017, https://www.technologyreview.com/2017/06/16/151178/ant-financial-chinas-giant-of-mobile-payments-is-rethinking-finance-with-ai/.
3. Will Knight, "Meet the Chinese Finance Giant That's Secretly an AI Company," *MIT Technology Review*, June 16, 2017, https://www.technologyreview.com/2017/06/16/151178/ant-financial-chinas-giant-of-mobile-payments-is-rethinking-finance-with-ai/.
4. Juliette van Winden, "Love at First Chat, with Lemonade's AI Chatbot Maya," Medium, December 1, 2019, https://medium.com/marketing-in-the-age-of-digital/love-at-first-chat-with-lemonades-ai-chatbot-maya-7b4a105824bd.
5. Jared Diamond, *Guns, Germs, and Steel: The Fates of Human Societies* (New York: W. W. Norton, 1997), 259.

Chapter 2

1. "Strategy Analytics: Half the World Owns a Smartphone," Business Wire, June 24, 2021, https://www.businesswire.com/news/home/20210624005926/en/Strategy-Analytics-Half-the-World-Owns-a-Smartphone.

2. Hilary George-Parkin, "One nation, on hold," Vox, May 13, 2020, https://www.vox.com/the-goods/2020/5/13/21243420/call-centers-on-hold-customer-service-unemployment-airline-cable.

Chapter 3

1. "Gartner Forecasts Worldwide Hyperautomation-Enabling Software Market to Reach Nearly $600 Billion by 2022," Gartner, April 28, 2021, https://www.gartner.com/en/newsroom/press-releases/2021-04-28-gartner-forecasts-worldwide-hyperautomation-enabling-software-market-to-reach-nearly-600-billion-by-2022.
2. Marco Iansiti and Karim R. Lakhani, "Competing in the Age of AI: How Machine Intelligence Changes the Rules of Business," *Harvard Business Review*, January–February 2020, https://hbr.org/2020/01/competing-in-the-age-of-ai.
3. Eric Jing, "Eric Jing on the Promise of Financial Services for the Unbanked," *Wall Street Journal*, January 17, 2018, https://www.wsj.com/articles/eric-jing-on-the-promise-of-financial-services-for-the-unbanked-1516200702.
4. Marco Iansiti and Karim R. Lakhani, "Competing in the Age of AI," *Harvard Business Review*, January–February 2020, https://hbr.org/2020/01/competing-in-the-age-of-ai.
5. "How to build AI with (and for) everyone in your organization," McKinsey & Company, May 4, 2020, https://www.mckinsey.com/business-functions/mckinsey-analytics/our-insights/how-to-build-ai-with-and-for-everyone-in-your-organization.

Chapter 4

1. Judith Shulevitz, "Siri, You're Messing Up a Generation of Children," *The New Republic*, April 2, 2014, https://newrepublic.com/article/117242/siris-psychological-effects-children.
2. James Crowley, "Woman Says Amazon's Alexa Told Her to Stab Herself in the Heart for 'The Greater Good,'" *Newsweek*, December 24, 2019, https://www.newsweek.com/amazon-echo-tells-uk-woman-stab-herself-1479074.
3. Karen Hao, "We read the paper that forced Timnit Gebru out of Google. Here's what it says," *MIT Technology Review*, December 4, 2020, https://

www.technologyreview.com/2020/12/04/1013294/google-ai-ethics-research-paper-forced-out-timnit-gebru/.

4. Jessica Nordell, quoted in Megan Thompson, "A new book examines ways to end unconscious bias," PBS NewsHour, September 18, 2021, https://www.pbs.org/newshour/show/a-new-book-examines-ways-to-end-unconscious-bias.

5. Jared Diamond, *Guns, Germs, and Steel: The Fates of Human Societies.* (New York: W. W. Norton, 1997), 30.

6. Michelle Lau, "We all have a 'hierarchy of needs.' But is technology meeting them?," World Economic Forum, July 2, 2019, https://www.weforum.org/agenda/2019/07/is-technology-meeting-our-fundamental-human-needs/.

CHAPTER 5

1. Tyler Clifford, "Coronavirus has ushered in the 'death of the call center,' LivePerson CEO says," CNBC, updated May 12, 2020, https://www.cnbc.com/2020/05/11/coronavirus-ushered-in-the-death-of-the-call-center-liveperson-ceo.html.

2. Katie Canales, "China's 'social credit' system ranks citizens and punishes them with throttled internet speeds and flight bans if the Communist Party deems them untrustworthy," *Business Insider*, updated December 24, 2021, https://www.businessinsider.com/china-social-credit-system-punishments-and-rewards-explained-2018-4.

3. Megan160 in Tucson, AZ, "I will no longer post a bad review about a guest," Community Center, Airbnb, October 15, 2017, https://community.with-airbnb.com/t5/Hosting/I-will-no-longer-post-a-bad-review-about-a-guest/td-p/526567.

4. Walter Isaacson, "How to Fix the Internet," *The Atlantic*, December 15, 2016, https://www.theatlantic.com/technology/archive/2016/12/how-to-fix-the-internet/510797/.

5. Shai Wininger, "The Secret Behind Lemonade's Instant Insurance," n.d., accessed February 18, 2022, https://www.lemonade.com/blog/secret-behind-lemonades-instant-insurance/.

6. Seth Grimes, "Unstructured Data and the 80 Percent Rule," Breakthrough Analysis, August 1, 2008, http://breakthroughanalysis.com/2008/08/01/unstructured-data-and-the-80-percent-rule/.

7. Chris Grams, "How Much Time Do Developers Spend Actually Writing Code?," The New Stack, October 15, 2019, https://thenewstack.io/how-much-time-do-developers-spend-actually-writing-code/.

CHAPTER 10

1. Hank Barnes, "Fusion Teams—A Critical Area for Vendors to Develop Understanding," LinkedIn Pulse, June 23, 2021, https://www.linkedin.com/pulse/fusion-teams-critical-area-vendors-develop-hank-barnes/.
2. Bayrhammer Klaus, "You spend much more time reading code than writing code," Medium, November 22, 2020, https://bayrhammer-klaus.medium.com/you-spend-much-more-time-reading-code-than-writing-code-bc953376fe19.

CHAPTER 11

1. "Worldwide Spending on Artificial Intelligence Is Expected to Double in Four Years, Reaching $110 Billion in 2024, According to New IDC Spending Guide," International Data Corporation, August 25, 2020, https://www.idc.com/getdoc.jsp?containerId=prUS46794720.
2. Hugo Britt, "Take a Look Under the Hood of Ford's Best Supply Chain Practices," Thomas Insights, July 22, 2020, https://www.thomasnet.com/insights/ford-supply-chain/.
3. Ben Goertzel, "Decentralized AI," TEDxBerkeley, April 23, 2019, video, 16:17, https://www.youtube.com/watch?v=r4manxX5U-0.

CHAPTER 12

1. "Fundamentals," IBM Design for AI, last updated May 2019, ibm.com/design/ai/fundamentals.
2. Cliff Saran, "Stanford University finds that AI is outpacing Moore's Law," Computer Weekly, December 12, 2019, https://www.computerweekly.com/news/252475371/Stanford-University-finds-that-AI-is-outpacing-Moores-Law.

CHAPTER 13

1. Eliot Van Buskirk, "Flowchart: Should You Buy a Pan Flute?" *Wired*, June 7, 2008, https://www.wired.com/2008/06/flowchart-shoul/.

CHAPTER 14

1. John H. Miller and Scott E. Page, *Complex Adaptive Systems: An Introduction to Computational Models of Social Life* (Princeton, NJ: Princeton University Press, 2009), 239.

CHAPTER 15

1. Susan Weinschenk, "Why Having Choices Makes Us Feel Powerful," *Psychology Today*, January 24, 2013, https://www.psychologytoday.com/us/blog/brain-wise/201301/why-having-choices-makes-us-feel-powerful.
2. Starbucks, "Top six ways to customize your favorite Starbucks drink," April 08, 2019, https://stories.starbucks.com/press/2019/customizing-beverages-at-starbucks-stores/.
3. Jaya Saxena, "Starbucks Stands by Its Most Annoying Customers and Their Wild Custom Drinks, Eater, May 5, 2021, https://www.eater.com/2021/5/5/22420813/starbucks-annoying-customized-drinks.
4. Arthur Van de Oudeweetering, *Improve Your Pattern Recognition: Key Moves and Motifs in the Middlegame* (Alkmaar, Netherlands: New in Chess, 2014).
5. RZA, "RZA on Chess and Bobby Fischer: Every game is a draw until you make a mistake," Lex Fridman Podcast, YouTube, 1:32, October 8, 2021, https://www.youtube.com/watch?v=uX0OzHkQlXI.
6. RZA, "Reflections of a King," Interview by Adisa "the Bishop" Banjoko, *Chess Life* magazine, January 2021, quoted by Adisa Banjoko, "A Conversation with RZA from the Wu-Tang Clan," US Chess Federation, January 5, 2021, https://new.uschess.org/news/conversation-rza-wu-tang-clan.

CHAPTER 16

1. Nadine Epstein, "Interview: Richard Saul Wurman: In Search of the God of Understanding," *Moment Magazine*, October 4, 2013, https://momentmag.com/ted-richard-saul-wurman-interview/.
2. Richard Saul Wurman, "The 5 Ways to Organize Information," video, 1:34, May 13, 2019, https://www.youtube.com/watch?v=Ak6nIJHlRcA.
3. Cathy Pearl, *Designing Voice User Interfaces: Principles of Conversational Experiences* (O'Reilly Media, 2016).
4. Erika Hall, *Conversational Design* (*A Book Apart,* 2018).

About the Authors

Robb Wilson

Robb Wilson is the founder, lead designer, and chief technologist behind OneReach.ai, the highest-scoring company in Gartner's first Critical Capabilities for Enterprise Conversational AI Platforms report and a leader for Completeness of Vision and Ability to Execute in Gartner's inaugural 2022 Magic Quadrant for Enterprise Conversational AI Platforms. Raised under the tutelage of philosopher Marshall McLuhan—who predicted the Internet 30 years before it became reality—Robb has spent more than two decades applying his deep understanding of user-centric design to unlocking hyperautomation. He built *UX Magazine* into the world's largest experience design publication while simultaneously creating Effective UI, a full-service UX firm that competed with IDEO and Frog Design. In addition to launching 15 startups and collecting over 130 awards across the fields of design and technology, Robb has held executive roles at several publicly traded companies and mentored colleagues who went on to leadership roles at Amazon Alexa, Google, Ogilvy, GE, Salesforce, Instagram, LinkedIn, Disney, Microsoft, Mastercard, and Boeing. Robb puts the same passion into building a surfboard and renovating his home that he instills in the start-ups he routinely bootstraps without venture or third-party capital. A trusted thought leader in the realm of conversational AI and hyperautomation, Robb has played a part in creating a wide variety of products, apps, and movies that have touched nearly every person on the planet. Robb is also a humble husband, father, and grandfather, and reading this bio always makes him blush a bit.

Josh Tyson

Josh Tyson is an author and producer who has held leadership roles for a variety of organizations, including TEDxMileHigh and *UX Magazine*. He is the co-host of N9K, a comedy podcast from the future. His writing has appeared in numerous publications over the years, including *Big*

Brother Skateboarding, Chicago Reader, FLAUNT, The New York Times, SLAP, Stop Smiling, Thrasher, and *Westword.* Josh lives with his family in Denver, where he enjoys skateboarding, yoga, and getting his kids to watch the weirdest films they can find on the Criterion Channel.

Index

Page numbers followed by *f* indicate a figure.

YOU'VE FINISHED READING THIS BOOK, BUT WE'RE NOT FINISHED WRITING IT!

Join the ongoing conversation beyond these pages.

YOU UNDERSTAND THE URGENCY, SCOPE, AND IMPACT OF CONVERSATIONAL AI AND HYPERAUTOMATION. YOU'RE READY TO SURGE AHEAD AND WANT MORE INFORMATION, TOOLS, AND BEST PRACTICES!!

Visit INVISIBLEMACHINES.AI for:

- Continued explorations of the key concepts in the book
- Illuminating and actionable case studies
- Conversations with Robb Wilson and other thought leaders in this space
- An ever-expanding library of artifacts, templates, and tools
- A gateway to important innovations in design and technology

VISIT INVISIBLEMACHINES.AI